EXEMPLARY LIFE

SCOTT BROWN

Exemplary Life
Copyright © 2024 by Scott Brown

Published by Lucid Books in Houston, TX
www.LucidBooks.com

All rights reserved. No part of this publication may be reproduced, stored in a retrieval system, or transmitted in any form by any means, electronic, mechanical, photocopy, recording, or otherwise, without the prior permission of the publisher, except as provided for by USA copyright law.

Unless otherwise indicated, scripture quotations are taken from the (NASB®) New American Standard Bible®, Copyright © 1960, 1971, 1977, 1995, 2020 by The Lockman Foundation. Used by permission. All rights reserved. www.lockman.org

ISBN: 978-1-63296-643-8
eISBN: 978-1-63296-644-5

Special Sales: Most Lucid Books titles are available in special quantity discounts. Custom imprinting or excerpting can also be done to fit special needs. Contact Lucid Books at Info@LucidBooks.com

And He has said to me, "My grace is sufficient for you, for power is perfected in weakness."

Most gladly, therefore, I will rather boast about my weakness so that the power of Christ may dwell in me.

—2 Cor. 12:9 (NASB 1995)

TABLE OF CONTENTS

Foreword	vii
Chapter 1	1
Chapter 2	3
Chapter 3	9
Chapter 4	13
Chapter 5	17
Chapter 6	22
Chapter 7	28
Chapter 8	30
Chapter 9	34
Chapter 10	37
Chapter 11	44
Chapter 12	47
Chapter 13	49
Chapter 14	52
Chapter 15	56
Chapter 16	62
Chapter 17	64
Chapter 18	67
Chapter 19	72
Chapter 20	75
Chapter 21	79

Chapter 22	83
Chapter 23	89
Chapter 24	94
Chapter 25	96
Chapter 26	100
Chapter 27	104
Chapter 28	109
Chapter 29	114
Chapter 30	120
Chapter 31	128
Chapter 32	131
Chapter 33	137
Chapter 34	140
Chapter 35	151
Chapter 36	153
Chapter 37	156
Chapter 38	158
Chapter 39	161
Chapter 40	167
Chapter 41	170
Chapter 42	173
Chapter 43	179
Chapter 44	192
A Message To My Fellow Christians	195
Epilogue	198
Reflection Section	213

FOREWORD

Many of you are familiar with the adage, "Into each life some rain must fall." The Bible underscores this truth in Acts 14:22 (NASB 1995), "Through many tribulations we must enter the kingdom of God." But very few people have experienced greater trials or more crushing blows than Scott Brown who, in a life-altering moment, lost almost everything he once held dear. Even fewer people come through such devastation with the ability to see it as a gift from God. Still, such is the life story of this courageous man and his seemingly innocent battle with an addiction that holds the power to destroy his life.

I am privileged to have walked this journey with Scott as his hometown pastor in Decatur, Illinois. Scott and his family were members of our church, St. Paul's Lutheran Church. I knew exactly where they all sat every Sunday, late service. I knew the solid reputation Scott and his wife were building as public school educators in our community and the growing respect Scott was developing as a junior high and high school coach. Like many in our community, I was devastated to learn of his arrest and later conviction, yet like few, I dared to believe that our God was bigger than the painful circumstances about to unfold.

I am doubly honored to introduce you to his story—his journey of faith—that will make you cry and make you angry but most of all will encourage you to trust a gracious God who specializes in bringing good out of evil and promises that nothing in all creation can separate us from His love.

EXEMPLARY LIFE

Though I have lived this journey with Scott, I couldn't believe how powerfully his story unfolds when I read his book. I found myself unable to put it down and marveled at the insights he pieces together of some of the seemingly insignificant details of this most shocking story, recognizing them all as a part of God's plan. To be living the American dream one moment with a new house, great career, fine family, great church, and wonderful friends, to sitting alone in a jail cell hours later is difficult to get your mind around. This is Scott's story, and he has lived to tell about it with great humility and courageous faith.

I hope that you as a reader will discover the truth of one of my favorite sayings, "God never wastes a hurt." Even in life's deepest valley, God is at work—no, especially in life's deepest valley. Here is where God works as the potter to mold and shape a lump of clay that has been softened by the storms of adversity, preparing it for a greater and more noble purpose. This book is part of a shared faith vision that our God consistently used the failures of some of his most trusted servants to become their most powerful life stories. Consider Moses, David, Peter, Paul, and, yes, even Scott. I know he is too humble and would never place himself next to these great heroes, but the same God was at work in each of these lives.

I'm excited to see how God will use this book going forward. Already many hearts have been touched, and I pray many more who live with secret sins growing in their hearts will find the courage and strength to willingly and openly lay it all down before a Savior who died for all sins and all sinners.

Thank you, Scott, for faithfully walking this often painful journey with faith and patience, always looking to Jesus, the Author and Perfecter of our faith.

FOREWORD

Thank you for doing the hard work of putting your story down on paper and believing God will use it to bless many others. Thank you for letting me be a small part of the mighty work of God in your heart and life.

God's richest and best to you and Michelle, as you are part of His unfolding story.

All for His glory.

> *It is not those who are healthy who need a physician, but those who are sick. . . . I did not come to call the righteous, but sinners.*
> —Jesus (Matt. 9:12–13 NASB 1995)

Pastor Wray Offermann
Retired Pastor
St. Paul's Lutheran Church

CHAPTER 1

One of my sons had just turned eight the day I got arrested, and my other son was a week away from turning 11. When I was released from prison, they were 13 and 16. This consequence of my imprisonment—a multiyear absence from the lives of my two sons—guaranteed that they would grow up just as I had, without a father in the home. These missing years are a relational abyss, a gaping hole that I dug for my family and a hole into which I unwittingly pushed my two sons due to my irresponsibility.

Twelve months before I was to be released from federal prison, I began writing this book in hopes it would help others avoid making the same stupid decisions I made. I had been arrested for ignoring something important and inserting something in its place that, in retrospect, was unimportant. I was charged and plead guilty in a federal court in front of a federal judge, and then I was sentenced to more prison time than anyone who knew the details of my case ever thought I would receive.

Though I battle daily with the consequences of my actions, I also know this: prison saved me. If I had not been sentenced to prison, I am sure I would be going to hell. And worse, I would have been racing to the fires, not even knowing that I was choosing hell.

I would have been one of the many souls completely surprised by my destination.

Thank you for reading my story. I'm holding nothing back, including the inner workings of our justice system and the people who shared in my journey. I hope my story keeps at least one of you from ever losing your family due to making the same careless choices I made.

It isn't worth it. Separation from those you love is never, ever worth it.

Finally, I must confess that because of my choices I feel I have lived three lives. My first life lasted more than 42 years. My second life was spent in a place you would never want to live, and that life I have detailed in this book. My third life—well, my third life I am confident will endure for all eternity.

CHAPTER 2

Although I was blessed in my first life, statistically I should have failed. Growing up in the '60s and '70s with a single parent seems to lower my odds of success.

In my first life, though, I had made it. I was married for 14 years, had two sons I adored, and owned two nice cars. I had a brand-new house surrounded by cornfields. I spent my weekdays teaching and coaching. On Saturdays I shuttled my sons to whatever sport they were playing. Sundays began with going to church and ended with tucking the boys into bed with prayers.

But my first life ended on a sunny July day when a line of seven police cars turned down my street and snaked toward my house.

It was 5:30 in the afternoon, and I was busy cutting wood to build a shed. I was a teacher by profession, but the building business I had purchased two years earlier was flourishing. Teaching paid the bills; the summer building paid for vacations and fun. Over the previous three summers, our family had enjoyed two trips to Disney World and one to Branson, Missouri. I was spoiling my sons, and I admit that these family vacations were what I had always yearned for as a youth but never experienced.

EXEMPLARY LIFE

Just as I finished cutting a section of boards, my wife called me to come to the middle of the front yard. She was concerned about the color, or texture, of the waste pile produced by our lovable maltipoo dog, Dash. It was a typical family discussion.

As I walked toward my wife, she asked if I thought Dash was okay, but my attention was drawn to the far edge of the block. A line of police cars was rounding the corner. Slowly and methodically, they moved at less than 10 miles per hour. As the vehicles crept closer, little did I know that my first life would end less than two minutes later.

As the mix of city police and county sheriff cars continued down the block, my wife and I had one of the last conversations of our 20-plus-year history as a couple. "Look at that," I said, wondering why so many police cars would suddenly appear on our street.

"Wow! I sure hope they're not coming here," my wife replied.

"They're probably going to Cory's for a surprise birthday or something," I told her. Of the 40 houses in the neighborhood, seven were occupied by families where the man of the house was a city police officer. Cornfields surrounded our subdivision. There was only one road, and it was created in the shape of a backward question mark.

Cory was a detective, and a surprise party with some from the local police force made perfect sense to me. Besides, there were no sirens or flashing lights, and the little cop convoy was moving at a friendly, perhaps ominous pace.

As the parade seemed to pass, they suddenly turned and stopped at our house—three cars in front, three on the side, and one on the corner. Then all seven doors opened, and more than seven uniformed officers marched toward my wife and me in the front yard.

I will never forget my wife's question. "What did you do?"

I replied, "Nothing. I don't know."

CHAPTER 2

I looked at the approaching officers, noting their size and then scanning each face. I quickly realized that I did not know any of them. One turned out to be the younger brother of a girl from my Lutheran grade school class, but I had not seen him in years. None of the rest of these guys looked familiar, and none of them were from the neighborhood.

The two guys who led the maneuver were not in uniform, and both carried items in their hands. The larger of the two held what looked like a laptop computer. He was just over six feet tall. The other man was much less than six feet tall and could not have weighed even 170 pounds. But he was not going to let his size dictate his position. He was in charge of this operation.

The shorter guy was Detective Welker. He was carrying what looked like a handful of paperwork and walked right up to me.

Detective Welker: "Are you Mr. Brown?"

Me: "Yes."

Detective Welker: "I have a search warrant for your house. You are under investigation for possession of child pornography. Where is your computer located?"

Me: "It's in the basement."

Me to my wife: "I don't have any of that."

Detective Welker to my wife: "Are your children home?"

My wife: "Yes."

Detective Welker: "Do you have somewhere you can take them for a few minutes?"

My wife walked into the house and walked the boys out the front door and to her sister's house, which was three houses away.

Detective Welker: "You stay here, Mr. Brown."

The larger officer and Detective Welker entered my house through the garage. I was left in my garage, surrounded by seven police officers who were investigating me for a crime I was sure I had not committed.

EXEMPLARY LIFE

No one spoke, and all the officers just stared at me. I was sure they were waiting for me to do something stupid—like run. But there was no reason to run. All of this would indeed work out. After I asked their permission, the police officers allowed me to busy myself by cleaning up the wood scraps on my driveway.

After about ten minutes, Detective Welker returned to the garage and called me over. He asked me to turn around and then handcuffed me and told me I was under arrest for possession of child pornography. He led me to a car, placed me in the back seat, and shut the door. I did not realize it then, but my first life—everything I had worked for—had just ended.

* * *

Upon arriving at the police station, I was placed in a small room with a camera (which turned out to be a blessing), a table, and two chairs. I had never been in an interrogation room before, but I had seen them on TV. This room was bright, comfortable, and spotless. My hands were free, and I was left to sit there. It wasn't like what I remembered on TV.

Detective Welker came in, and unlike in the garage, he now seemed very friendly and polite. He asked me if I wanted to talk about what was happening. I told him I did because this was a mistake, and I just wanted to go home. He informed me that I was not going home tonight. I was under arrest and would need to talk to the judge about going home. He then asked if I wanted something to drink. I requested a Pepsi, and he brought an ice cold one right away.

Detective Welker sat down, and we had a friendly little chat. He again asked me if I would like to talk and informed me that our conversation may be recorded. I don't know if he recorded all

CHAPTER 2

of his interrogation, but it would later turn out to my benefit, not his, that he recorded this one.

Have you ever had a life-changing moment you can never forget? Well, this was one of mine. I can recall our brief conversation almost word for word to this day. Here is the condensed version from the interrogation videotape.

Detective Welker: "How long have you been downloading child pornography?"

Me: "I've been downloading adult pornography for probably five years, but I don't search for child pornography."

Detective Welker: "What search terms do you use?"

Me: "I don't know. If I find a video I like, I search the terms connected to it to see if I can find more like it."

Detective Welker: "Like what terms do you use?"

Me: "Usually I use the term *new porn* because after five years I am convinced I have seen all of them. I usually get repeats now. I have not even been on there for probably two weeks. I also used the phrase *small boobs* because I like small boobs like my wife has. We met when she was 19 and I was 22, and I've looked online for girls that look like her. I found some good videos called 'Long Island Lolitas,' so I've searched for *lolitas*."

Detective Welker: "Lolitas is a code word for child porn."

Me: "I didn't know that. I was getting the Long Island Lolita stuff."

Detective Welker: "So, Mr. Brown, how long have you been collecting child pornography?"

Me: "I don't collect it. I had seen it come through when I downloaded adult pornography, but I have never watched it. I hit the X and delete it when I see that stuff come up. You can only preview maybe half of the videos. If I preview one with kids in it, I don't download it."

Detective Welker: "How many videos do you have on your computer?"

Me: "I don't know. I don't save them. Maybe 50 or so from the last time I searched. I have not been back on there to see what they are."

Detective Welker: "Mr. Brown, you have over 400 videos on your computer."

Me: "Child stuff?"

Detective Welker: "I don't know yet. We are still going through them. How many child pornography videos do you think you have?"

Me: "I don't know. I thought I had maybe 50 total videos. You are telling me I have 400. I have no idea how many are child pornography."

And with that, our friendly little conversation ended. I again asked if I could go home. Detective Welker told me I was under arrest, and it would be up to the judge to decide if I would be released. I was led out of the little room and to my cell. Thus began my second life.

CHAPTER 3

My little cell had a metal bunk with a very thin mattress. There was also a toilet. That was it. After the door closed, I remember burying my face in my hands and crying. All the stuff I relied upon—my cell phone, my wallet, and my clothes—had been taken from me, and now all I had was my jail-issued jumpsuit.

I knew there were other little rooms like mine along the wall, but I had no idea how many were occupied. By this time, it was about 10:00 p.m., and most of the lights were off. There was no noise from the other cells or in the hallway.

All night I sat or laid down on my bunk praying to God. I remember repeating the words "God help me" over and over. I do not remember going to sleep. Often I thought about my sons and cried. I was not able to tuck them in tonight. I was not able to say prayers with them tonight. I could not check on them in the middle of the night when I heard a noise. I was stuck here, and they did not have me as a dad.

The lights popped on at about 6:00 a.m., and my cell door opened. A few minutes later, another inmate came to my door with a mop and asked if I wanted my room cleaned. I said no and just sat on my bunk. He informed me that I had to take my mattress off my bed and sit outside the cell for breakfast. I complied by moving to the wall outside my cell.

I could not believe what I saw. About 25 other guys were milling around, watching the little corner TV, or playing cards. Everyone I saw looked comfortable. I just sat in my corner.

When the call came for breakfast, we were all supposed to go to the control window and get our trays. I just sat there.

After about three minutes, a young black guy brought my tray over and told me I should eat something. I thanked him for the tray and asked him how and when I would be able to make a phone call. He just walked away.

He returned about five minutes later and handed me a phone card. He told me he only had about 20 minutes left on the card and to try to make my call quickly.

That was amazing. I had never seen this guy—a criminal—before in my life. He was in jail like me, but he saw a need and helped me.

I made a call to my house, and nobody answered. So I tried my in-laws. My father-in-law answered and told me that his wife and my wife were at the courthouse to bail me out.

Breakfast ended sometime during that call, and I was allowed to sit back in my little corner of the jail.

It struck me as odd that all the other guys there had a carefree attitude. They were going about life as if nothing was wrong. Later I realized this attitude was because for many of these guys, jail was a revolving door.

I wondered if my sons were awake yet and what they were doing. They were probably running around the house in their cartoon pajamas, watching TV, eating cereal, and not knowing anything was wrong with daddy. I had always been there for them. I will be coming home soon.

CHAPTER 3

I don't know how long I sat on that jail floor. But the same young guy who had brought me my breakfast tray returned and asked me if I was finished. I had taken a couple of bites of the hard-boiled egg. I can't tell you what else was on the tray. He returned my tray to the window. I never saw him again. I hope he came out okay.

After about 30 minutes, a guard called my name along with some others to go before the judge. It was the express line today. I walked in, and the acting prosecutor read the charge and asked for $40,000 bail. The judge had a surprised look on his face. He looked at something on his desk and then announced that it was much too high for a first-time offender with no criminal record. He put my bail at $20,000, and I left the courtroom. The entire episode took about one minute.

When the guard brought me back to the hallway, two other prisoners were talking about their bail. One was griping that his $500 bail was too high when all they had found on him was a "little bit of stuff." I don't know what the "stuff" was.

The other prisoner agreed and then turned to me. He asked me what my bail was. I said $20,000, and they both got giant eyes. I will edit what the first guy said, but it was on the lines of "Holy Batman! What did you do?" I just looked at the floor and said I did not want to talk about it. That was the end of the conversation.

Some guards walked all of us back to the common room. I took my place back on the floor, back against the wall. I was there about 10 minutes when I noticed a young white guy staring at me from about 15 feet away.

Finally, he said, "How you doing, Coach Brown?"

I had been known as Coach Brown for the last 14 years. Every kid that came through my gym called me that. Here was one of my former students in the same jail with me. I could not place his name. His face, older now, was a little bit familiar.

I just looked at him and said, "I'm okay."

I began to think of all the kids I had coached over the years. Then I went back to thinking about my two sons. They had to be finished with breakfast and watching TV by now. They would be sitting on the couch. The older one would be clutching his stuffed bear, Blue-Berry. My younger son would be doing the same with Sunny-Bear. And I was not at my place, sitting between them as I always did on lazy Saturday mornings.

At some point, a guard appeared at the gate and called my name. He told me I had been bailed out. I went to a little room and changed out of my jumpsuit into my own clothes.

A guard led me to the waiting room. There I found my wife, her mother, and my best friend, Mike. I grabbed my wife and just held onto her for some time. I shook my friend's hand and thanked him for coming. Likewise, I thanked my mother-in-law.

My friend asked no questions. He was there because he was my friend. My mother-in-law was there for her daughter.

On the way home, my wife and I talked as her mom drove. I explained everything. My wife knew I had watched pornography on the computer. That was no secret. We discussed hiring a lawyer who was a friend of mine. He would be able to sort all this out. It was, after all, unintentional. We were on our way home to figure out a plan.

CHAPTER 4

When we got home, I hugged both of my sons and held them for a long time. They did not understand what was happening. We all ate lunch and once again were the perfect all-American family. Daddy was home.

After lunch, I went out to the driveway to clean up the wood and sawdust from the day before. A little red car pulled up. Another log was about to be thrown on the fire.

A tiny lady who looked to be in her late 50s came walking up the driveway, striding right for me. I greeted her and asked if I could help her.

She stopped six feet short of me, looked me dead in the eyes, and said, "Who are you?"

Understand that this occurred in my driveway, at my house, and in my neighborhood. And this woman neither smiled nor greeted me. She just looked me in the eyes and with a sense of authority asked, "Who are you?"

I responded with my name. She pulled out her cell phone so fast that it looked like she was doing a quick draw in the Wild Wild West, and I was about to be shot in the gut. Before I recognized what was happening, she had unsnapped the holder, flipped it open, and had her index finger pointed at what I now imagine was a shortcut key to her home base.

She immediately asked, "Where are your sons?" Her voice was getting louder and more aggressive. Did I mention that she was just short of 5 feet tall and had likely never seen 90 pounds in her life?

I responded that my sons were inside watching TV. She identified herself as being from the Department of Children and Family Services (DCFS) and said I was not supposed to be there on my driveway or at my house.

With her pointer finger poised just above the magic button on her phone, she said that if I did not leave the premises right then, she would "call the police and have them remove my children to foster care." I put that in quotes because those are words I will never forget.

What happened next amounted to a 60-second scramble. I did not want her to push that button any more than I would have wanted her to shoot me. I told her I would need to go in and get my truck keys. She told me I was not going into the house, or she would call the police. Her pointer finger was twitching dangerously close to the phone.

I yelled for my wife, who came out of the house. I quickly told her what was happening. I emphasized that this lady was there to take our sons to foster care. My wife ran back in to get my truck keys. She gave them to me, and I walked down the drive to my truck. I left her there with the lady sent to protect our children. As I drove away from the house, tears for my sons flowed down my cheeks.

When I phoned my wife later, I learned that DCFS had put a "no contact" order on me regarding my own sons. She said the lady explained that they do this in these cases to ensure the kids are safe. She advised my wife that under no circumstances was I to

CHAPTER 4

have any contact with my sons—even with my wife present. If my wife let me see my sons, DCFS would immediately come and take my sons from my wife and place them in foster care.

I found out sometime later that DCFS does not, in fact, do this in every case. I could not understand why they did this in my case. I thought back to the conversation I had with Detective Welker. I'd explained to him that this was all a mistake. I had told him the truth about what happened and had done so without even having my lawyer present. I can only guess that DCFS did not get an accurate account of what led to my arrest.

I strongly recommend that no one ever talk to a detective without having a lawyer present. I never will again. But in this case, it would work out for the best because my interrogation and later actions by Detective Welker were videotaped.

All I knew for sure was that I had been arrested for something I did not feel I had done intentionally. And due to these charges, the authorities were not letting me see my sons—the sons I love more than anything.

After I left my house, I made arrangements to stay with my best friend. I made phone calls on the way to his house. The phone call I remember the most was the one I made to my brother, Mark. I explained to Mark what had happened. It was a tear-filled conversation. A few parts of the exchange have stuck with me, and details that emerged from our chat pointed me to the problem. I told him that whenever I noticed that one of these illegal videos came through, I immediately deleted it. He explained that the videos were more than likely still on my computer. Mark explained that when I hit the delete key on the video player, it was not deleting the videos from my computer.

Several years ago, Mark had installed the program to download videos on my computer and had used it himself. I asked him if he still had that program. He did not. He said that

EXEMPLARY LIFE

a year earlier he was doing some downloading, and after a video was on his computer, he found it was an illegal child pornography video. He immediately knew the program was no longer safe and removed it and all the files from his computer. He was upset he did not call me to warn me about this. If he had warned me, I would never have lost my first life. But I would have never gained my third one either.

CHAPTER 5

That evening my wife and I talked on the phone. Due to the encounter with DCFS and a phone call she received from Detective Welker, she thought it would be a good idea for her and the boys to get out of town for a few days. It was July, and my wife and I still had a month of summer vacation before our teaching jobs began.

My wife's mother had made arrangements for her, my wife, and the boys to go to Louisiana. They would go away for a week or two and let things settle down.

My mother-in-law's best friend, Maria, worked as a counselor in the Bayou State and had even talked about hosting a Bible study at her house. I remember my wife saying that Maria would be able to help our family get through this. She would be the best bet for our family to remain strong in this trying time— or so I believed.

The one thing that concerned me about their trip was that I had never been away from my sons for more than two days. They planned to be away for at least a week.

My wife told me why she wanted to get out of town. Detective Welker advised her that my story would be in the newspaper and on television the next day. I had been a teacher and a coach for

14 years. I had won the County Volleyball Coach of the Year Award two years earlier. Throughout my career, I had contact with thousands of children and families. The detective told her this was going to be a big story. That turned out to be an understatement.

The next day, my arrest was the lead story on every news broadcast during the day. They showed a video archive of me in the gym, leading a lesson on the importance of physical fitness for children. As I stood near the gym wall, about 25 second graders were jogging, skipping, and hopping to the beat of the music. While this was going on, the reporter announced that I had been arrested for possession of child pornography. She briefly summarized my 14 years of teaching and coaching and listed the schools where I had served. After that, she reported my age, and then the screen changed to a video of my house. I couldn't believe the TV crew had filmed it at my house. Fortunately, nobody was home when they were there.

The following day, my wife called from her mother's house to let me know they were all packed and would be in the car in about one hour to head out of town. We decided I would drive over to my in-laws' house for goodbye hugs with my boys. This quick visit was a risky decision. DCFS had told my wife they would be watching. Although there were no allegations during my arrest that I had had inappropriate contact with any child, the agency threatened to take the boys to foster care immediately if they learned I had any contact with them. My wife and I were both fearful but decided to risk the short visit.

I drove to the area and parked across the street from my in-laws' house. I waited in a business parking lot until I saw my wife and sons come out of the house and get in their car. My phone rang, and in the spirit of an undercover operation, my wife just said, "Come now."

CHAPTER 5

I zipped over to the house, pulled in next to their car, and got out. My wife and I hugged for a short time before my oldest son took his turn. He climbed out of the car while my wife kept watch. He grabbed me with a strength that should not come from a 10-year-old. We were both crying.

I told him he would only be gone for about a week and that I would see him when he got home. He did not want to go. He couldn't get any words out but just sobbed and sobbed. Although he did not understand what was happening, not being with his daddy for a week seemed impossible.

My wife broke us apart and told my younger son, age eight, to say goodbye to his daddy. He was in the back seat of their car and wouldn't move. He focused on his handheld video game and would not look at me. This distance was not about the game but how he dealt with sadness. He was always the boy who did not want others to see him cry. Whenever something was wrong, he shut down. And that is what he did.

I climbed into the back seat of their car and said goodbye to him. I told him to have a good time on vacation and that I would see him when they returned. I told him I loved him and hugged him. His only response was to tip his head onto my shoulder.

My older son was standing outside the car, waiting. As I climbed out, he grabbed me and did not want to let go. I told him everything would be fine. My wife eventually interrupted and said they needed to go. Her motivation was absolute fear; I could see it in her eyes. She expected the authorities to fly around the corner, seven cars strong again, and steal the children off to foster care. I gave my wife one last hug, got in my truck, and drove away, barely able to see the road through my tears.

My wife and I agreed to talk by cell phone about every hour. I set the alarm on my watch, but that was not necessary. I watched the clock all day long.

One of the things we did on family road trips was buy scratch-off lottery tickets. On our way out of town, we would pull into a gas station to top off the tank and buy a few big tickets that would take some time to scratch off. I had bought some tickets earlier that morning. When my older son and I said goodbye, I presented him with those tickets for the trip.

My oldest son wanted to talk to me during one of the phone calls. He told me with a long, drawn-out, dramatic description how he had scratched off one of the tickets and won $20. I will never forget what he said next. "Dad, see that? God is taking care of us."

I was so proud of him. He had God firmly planted in his heart. We had taken both boys to church nearly every Sunday since they were born, and they loved Sunday school. I read stories to the boys from a children's Bible almost every night. I chuckled one evening when my younger son informed me that we were about to read through his Bible for the fifth time. I asked if he was getting tired of it. He wasn't.

How interesting it is that my oldest son was demonstrating what is known as "child-like faith." That is the all-trusting faith in God that He will get you through. And for three days I had been praying to God with so little faith. I thought I was going to handle this myself. I just needed Him to back me.

The drive to Louisiana went smoothly for my family. They arrived there that evening, and as planned, my wife and I talked nearly every hour. She shared where they were, what sights they had seen, and what the boys were doing. It was mostly small talk, but I felt it showed our love for each other was not in question. Well, in my mind, it wasn't.

That night at about 10:00 p.m., my wife and I chatted again before saying goodnight. The next morning, we spoke again. I was going to be meeting with my lawyer to discuss this issue and

CHAPTER 5

told my wife I would call her right after the meeting at around noon. But she never answered that arranged call. I called every half hour or so all day, but she never answered. Her phone was off. Something was wrong.

That night at about 7:00 p.m., my wife finally called. Relieved to see her number, I answered on the first ring. I started to say something about trying to reach her all day, but her words were like a knife to my heart. With ice in her voice, she said, "Listen. Maria knew you were guilty before we even got here. I want a divorce."

Our conversation confirmed that my first life was truly over, and my second life was continuing on an even faster downward spiral.

CHAPTER 6

It took me some time to comprehend what had changed my wife. I found it was a combination of four things that had given her the idea of divorce.

First, the police had been doing their "work." A neighbor who still believed in me told me that on Sunday while my family was traveling to Louisiana, a few officers who lived in my neighborhood went door to door.

Young families with school-age children dominated our little subdivision. On any given weekend, you could find 20 or more kids out riding their bikes, playing ball, or swinging on one of the mini-playgrounds in a backyard.

The officers came to a neighbor's house and told him why I had been arrested. They asked that he sit down with his two young children and find out if I had ever touched them inappropriately. The officers also informed him that they had "evidence" that there would be some kids "coming out of the woodwork" from the schools where I had taught. Talking to his children was not just suggested; according to the officers, it was necessary. My wife's sister and some friends in the neighborhood told my wife about these visits.

CHAPTER 6

The second factor that prompted my wife to consider divorce was a phone call she had with Detective Welker. My wife told me about the conversation, which I call the "six untruths." My lawyer has advised me not to call them what they actually were—a three-letter word that begins with "L" and rhymes with "die."

Detective Welker told my wife that the police had been "watching me for five years" (untruth number 1). I pointed out to my wife that it made no sense. Why would they let me continue to teach elementary through high school children for five years if they suspected something? Detective Welker got this five-year comment from my interview when I told him I had been downloading adult pornography for "about five years." He used this comment I made during the interrogation to convince my wife that I had been on their radar.

Detective Welker also told my wife they had "reason to believe there were going to be some children from my schools come out of the woodwork" to accuse me of molesting them (untruth number 2). I cried as I promised my wife I had never done that.

Detective Welker had more. He told my wife they had "evidence" that I had bought child pornography (untruth number 3). He wanted her to review our credit card records when she returned home. Again, I denied this to my wife. Later, she checked our credit card records and verified that I had never purchased any pornography.

He followed this up by telling her that they "suspected" I might have produced some child pornography (untruth number 4). When he served the search warrant at my house, he confiscated some VHS tapes along with my computer. The videotapes were labeled with girls' names on them. These "suspicious" tapes were on my computer desk.

When Detective Welker sat down to watch them, he found college recruitment tapes I had made for my most talented high school volleyball players over the years. These were the master copies we used to produce the recordings sent to college coaches. The tapes Detective Welker was referring to would be the very tapes that helped get a few of my players college scholarship offers. But of course, Detective Welker did not mention the content of these "suspicious" tapes to my wife.

The next thing I heard really stumped me. Detective Welker asked my wife if she had gained some weight recently. She replied that she had. He told her I said I was unhappy with her weight gain, which was why I was looking at pornography (untruth number 5). This one baffled me more than the rest. To my knowledge, my wife had not "gained weight recently." We had been together for over 20 years. She may have put on a few pounds since high school and had given birth to two beautiful boys. But "gained weight recently"? That is a loaded question. If you ask almost any woman that, what will she think? She may say no or yes, but her thought process after a question like that is less than favorable.

Now that Detective Welker had thoroughly upset my wife and undermined all feelings of trust and love my wife had for me, it was time for him to drive the nail in the coffin. He told my wife something she probably repeated to me almost word for word. My wife said she was supposed to talk to my sons to see if I had ever abused them because Detective Welker insisted there was a video on my computer with a title graphically depicting father-son sex. He told her the name of this video. I am intentionally leaving the disgusting title he gave that video out of this writing, but I remember what she told me word for word. Months later, using Detective Welker's own forensic report, we confirmed there were no illegal father-son videos on my computer, much less a video by that title (untruth number 6).

CHAPTER 6

At this point in the conversation with my wife, utter disbelief overcame me. I wondered how she could believe any of this. I had told her exactly what happened, and none of this made any sense. We had known each other for so long. Surely she knew me better than this.

When I met with my lawyer, Howard, the next day, I told him the six untruths Detective Welker had shared with my wife. With tears, I asked him why the detective would make up such awful, untrue things to tell my wife. Howard told me it is a common investigation practice. The detective wanted everyone against me. The thinking was that I would confess to everything when I was at my lowest and have no one to turn to.

I told my lawyer I had already confessed everything to Detective Welker. Howard knew this and was not happy about it. My concern now was that my family, especially my sons, would be part of the collateral damage of Detective Welker's biased investigation.

The third factor that led to our divorce was my wife's "great idea" visit to the counselor, Maria, in Louisiana. I had met Maria, my mother-in-law's friend, on four or five occasions throughout the years when she came to visit our family. She was always friendly enough, but it is clear now that Maria had decided to help my wife move on and not try to keep our family together.

My wife told me, "Maria knew you were guilty before we even got here. I want a divorce." Then she said, "You fit the profile."

I asked my wife, "What profile?" Maria had shown my wife a profile on the Internet of someone who might be a pedophile. It included middle-aged, white, educated males. Check. But this was the clincher. The profile mentioned that these people might have extensive toy collections.

I began collecting slot cars as a young boy in the 1960s and had accumulated over 600. Sharing that passion with my sons was incredible. We spent many evenings racing on the sizable four-lane track I had built. Before each of my sons hit second grade, they could put together a working slot car from parts. This hobby was one of our favorite father-son activities, especially during cold Illinois winters.

But Maria failed to tell my wife why a pedophile might collect toys. They do this to lure children to them. However, my collection and our track were for my sons and me to enjoy. In the four years we had the big racetrack, neighborhood kids only raced on it with my sons a few times. Maria chose to see my slot car collection as evidence to support her evaluation from hundreds of miles away. Remember, she "knew I was guilty" before my wife and sons ever got to Louisiana.

The next day, I talked to my pastor about this conversation. I was distraught and asked if I could meet with him. During the meeting, he asked me to tell him about Maria. I told him everything I knew. He made it all make sense.

My wife was vulnerable, and she looked to Maria for guidance. As a friend of the family and counselor, Maria had a choice. Taking one path, she could help my wife through this difficult time and discuss ways to deal with everything and be strong for our sons. Through that, she could help my wife salvage the marriage and our family.

Taking another path, Maria could help my wife distance herself from the complex and difficult situation and move on from her previous life. She could help her focus on making herself happy, regardless of the impact on her children, and do what seemed easier.

The first path allowed for an adjusted life. The second path allowed for a new beginning with a completely different life. My pastor asked me, "Which path changes your family's world?" It made sense. Maria thought she could more significantly impact my wife by encouraging her to create a new life for herself.

CHAPTER 6

My attitude during our marriage was the fourth factor that led to the divorce—specifically, my attitude toward my wife's appearance. She was not a large woman and could never be described as fat. But I picked on a few of her flaws. I had spent so much time looking at pornography that I had a false picture in my mind of what I thought my wife's body should look like.

Sometimes I patted her tummy and made a comment about it. I thought it was just a little reminder to watch her weight. I wasn't trying to be mean, but I didn't realize it was demeaning.

Sometimes my wife and I weren't intimate for a month or more. I was not physically attracted to my wife because, in my view, she was out of shape. I will never forget the one time I hurt her more than ever. We were lying in bed, and she asked me what was wrong. I told her I loved her very much but was not physically attracted to her. That thought makes me sick now. How I wish I could take back those words.

Let me tell you what I should have seen. I should have seen the wife who would have done anything for her husband and sons. I should have seen the wife who worked all day teaching and then came home and fixed fabulous meals. I should have seen the wife who listened whenever I wanted to talk about my great day or my bad day. I should have seen the wife who was proud to have a family and put her sons before everything. I should have seen the wife who was proud of her husband's accomplishments. I should have seen the wife who never tooted her own horn. And I should have seen my wife as the person who, no matter how many times I pointed out her "faults," she still loved me because I was her husband.

But I did not see any of that because I was too busy seeing that she did not look like the women in the adult videos. The effect of pornography on my thought process was the fourth factor and the driving force that led to our divorce.

CHAPTER 7

For two years before I was arrested, I had devoted less time to viewing pornography. But for three years before that, I was on the computer every night searching for videos I had not seen yet. I remember nights I was up until 3:00 a.m. trying to find new ones. Finally I was convinced I had seen all the videos out there, and by the time of my arrest, I was browsing only every few months.

I had not been on LimeWire, the file-sharing program I used, for a few months before my arrest. My wife used the same program to download music. One night, she went to the computer in the basement to download some music for her and my oldest son's new music players. She came back upstairs, told me what they were going to do, and asked me to get the porno videos off there so my son would not see them. I was confused about where she said they were, so she showed me. There in a file was what looked like an endless list of them. I was dumbfounded because I thought I had deleted most of what came onto the computer.

I called my brother, the IT guy who had installed LimeWire for me. I told him I had a bunch of videos in a file and was unsure what they were. I wanted to know how to move them so my wife could download music. He explained over the phone to

CHAPTER 7

do some click-and-drag moves. Then I wrote the new location for the videos on a piece of paper.

Later that night when I went down to the computer to continue searching for slot cars on eBay, I noticed in the lower corner of the screen that LimeWire was still running. I clicked on it, and it looked like my wife's songs were all done downloading. So I typed in the search term "new porn" and hit download. Like always, hundreds of possible matches came up on the screen. I clicked on the first 25 or 30, minimized the program like I always did, and went back to my eBay screen.

One of the videos the detective was fishing out that night on LimeWire was called "new child porn." I had clicked on it with all the rest and never gave it a second thought. I had opened the door for Detective Welker to search my computer.

And search my computer he did. Apparently, the file I moved with my brother's help contained over 400 videos. The detective's original forensic report stated that there were 26 confirmed illegal videos. My first life actually ended that night. I just did not know it yet.

Reflection Section for Chapters 1–7 available on page 213

CHAPTER 8

After my arrest, my wife and sons stayed in Louisiana for two weeks. A week after they arrived, my son had his 11th birthday. We talked on the phone a few times that day. He told me he wanted me there, and I assured him I wanted to be there and that we would celebrate his birthday again when they got home. It was heartbreaking to be separated for his birthday. Our family lived a blessed life, and we were always able to make birthdays a big deal.

I talked to my sons every day they were away. They shared what they were doing and told me about a movie they watched, about roller skating, and how they went on a shopping trip. It sounded like they were having fun, but they also shared with me some negative thoughts.

My older son confided in a hushed voice that Mommy told him I would never ever live with them again. I believe my wife had tried to share this with our sons gently. But my son also told me he did not like Grandma or Maria anymore. He said he was trying to watch TV the night they got there, but they sat at the table and talked about how Mommy was "going to get rid of Daddy."

I did not question my son about it. I just told him that Mommy was mad right now and that we were going to pray about it. So

CHAPTER 8

that night on the phone we said prayers together like we had done every night. I asked God to help us all work this out and to keep us safe. My oldest son asked God to let Mommy make up with Daddy so they could come home. I finished the prayer in heavy tears.

I tried to talk to my wife daily, but she became more distant and angry. I asked her what she had said to the boys, and she told me she was handling it. She explained to the boys that we both still loved them. I remember telling her that divorce was not what was best for the boys. I will never forget her response. She said, "Kids are resilient. They go through divorce every day and come out fine." I could write an entire book on that one thought and all that is wrong with it.

My wife began to do something very strange to me on the phone. Every conversation started calmly enough, but then she started yelling and hanging up the phone—literally, every conversation. We could be having a good talk, and suddenly it was like she realized she was letting her guard down. Once in the background I heard her mom say, "You need to hang up." My wife immediately started yelling at me and hung up. No goodbye. When I called her back to address what she had said, I realized she had shut off her phone.

I asked my counselor about that behavior, and he asked if I had ever abused my wife. I told him of course not. I loved her very much. He believed she had received abuse counseling from her counselor. That would be Maria.

When a spouse is abused, they are typically counseled to take control of their life. They are to give no respect or consideration to the abuser. The yelling and hanging up was my wife's way of gaining control of the conversation and ending it in her favor. This strategy is used when there is no hope of two people resolving their conflicts. As my counselor put it, the approach is used after general marriage counseling has failed. I guess Maria skipped that part.

My wife and sons stayed in Louisiana for 14 days. I spent my days working and going to counseling, and I spent my evenings with friends. I began counseling the Monday after my arrest. I met with my pastor at my church for about two hours. We talked about what had happened and why it had happened. He finished the session by giving me the name of a Christian counselor in our town who specialized in sexual addiction.

I made an appointment with Dr. Wentz and continued meeting with him weekly. About six months later, I started meeting with him every other week. He was very thorough in helping me understand my wife's point of view. He was also very helpful in working me through the hate I had for certain people involved in this. The characteristic I found the most beneficial, though, was his Christian background.

Everything he said was with the understanding that our family unit was in trouble. And when you face a crisis of that magnitude, you face it with prayer. Between him and my pastor, I began praying more than I had ever prayed. Prayer became my calming point. No matter what anyone threw at me, I knew I could go to God in prayer.

Dr. Wentz also became one of my biggest supporters. My attorney spoke with him before I went before the judge and determined he would be an excellent person to speak for me.. He was able to share his thoughts on my day of sentencing and was part of the reason I was given a very light sentence compared to what is prescribed for this crime.

My family's return from Louisiana was a stressful event. I agreed to leave the house before they got back to town. I packed my clothes and prepared to go back to my friend's house where I would be staying. I was scrambling to get out of the house when my wife called. She told me they would be home in about two hours and that I needed to get out of there in time. She did not want to see me.

CHAPTER 8

She also told me that when they got back to town, she had to go to DCFS. The caseworker wanted to talk to my sons. My wife explained that if she did not do this, I would not be able to see my boys.

My wife and sons went to DCFS the next day and met with a supervisor there. I will call her Angie. After that meeting, my wife dropped yet another bombshell on me.

She said the meeting went well. She told Angie I was the best father and had a great relationship with my sons. Angie then took both boys to another room. They returned within ten minutes, and Angie told my wife that everything was fine with the boys. However, she warned my wife not to let me see my sons. If she did, they would be placed in foster care.

I remember bursting into tears and asking my wife why. She had no idea. She said I was supposed to call Angie so she could tell me the arrangements that could be made so I could see them under certain circumstances. As soon as my wife and I hung up, I called Angie.

CHAPTER 9

Angie informed me that I could see my sons once a week for an hour at her office. If I wanted to see them more than that, I would need to make arrangements with one of their client supervisors. Hiring a supervisor would allow me to see my sons as much as I wanted as long as the supervisor was with me. Angie gave me the name of someone available for off hour visits. She then told me that this, by the way, would cost me $20 per hour.

I did not care about the cost. I called the phone number she gave me for the supervisor, and an older woman named Jeanie talked with me. She was available to observe me when I spent time with my sons. The earliest time that would work for all involved would be in two days, so we set up the meeting.

My wife did not want me to pick up the kids at our house. She said, "The neighbors do not want you out there." She also would not bring the kids to me because she did not want to see me. Instead, she drove my sons to her mother's house, and I picked them up there.

I met Jeanie at the gas station near my mother-in-law's house. Jeanie had the look of a friendly grandmother. She was only in her early 60s, but as a lifelong smoker, she did not have a sweet, grandmotherly voice.

CHAPTER 9

Jeanie climbed into my truck, said a short hello, and then looked me in the eyes and gave me the "rules." She told me not to engage in excessive hugging and warned me not to go where she could not be next to us. I wondered what she thought I had actually done.

She appeared weak at first glance, but I could tell she had frequently dealt with the lower end of the parenting scale. She told me she had seen it all and was prepared to protect my sons at all costs. I just nodded in disbelief. She allowed me to start my truck, and we drove the short trip to pick up my sons.

When we pulled into the driveway, the house door opened, and my boys came walking out. They had a somewhat unsure look on their faces. Mine was already covered in tears. Right behind them was my mother-in-law. Jeanie had done her duty and climbed out of the truck to observe our hug. She confirmed our return time with my mother-in-law, and we all got in the truck. The scene was set—one man and two boys in tears, and a grandma with an attitude, all off to make a day of it.

That visit was a blur. It lasted three hours, but it felt like three minutes. We ate at McDonald's, went to the park, and kicked the soccer ball. All the while, Jeanie was tagging along.

On our trip back to my mother-in-law's house, my older son began to ask a few questions. He wanted to know if Mom and I would be able to get back together and when we would see each other again. He also wanted to know what had happened to make Mom, Maria, and Grandma so mad. I explained nothing to him. I reminded him that I loved him and his brother and that God was watching over us. We pulled into the driveway, and the truck came to a stop. My oldest son then asked if we could say a prayer, so we did.

With tears in my eyes, I drove Jeanie back to the gas station. I paid her the $60 we had agreed on for her three hours of work.

She reminded me that I should not say anything to my sons about my case. Then she softened her look. She told me she did not know what I did, but it was clear to her that there was a love between my sons and me that she had not seen between parent and child in a long time. So I told her what I had done, and we sat talking in the truck for an extra hour. She did not charge me another $20.

Over the next four months, Jeanie became a friend. I visited with my sons on two or three weekdays and for six hours on Sundays. Jeanie watched my sons and I go roller skating, play video games, kick the soccer ball, and throw the football. She watched us play tag, wrestle, and laugh about anything and everything. On occasion, she also watched us cry. I shared with her what was happening in my case, and she became my huge supporter.

Jeanie also shared things about her own life. She was single and had recently filed for bankruptcy. The money I was paying her was allowing her to pay her bills. She had also been in and out of church during her life. We spent some of our time talking about the Bible. We talked about the church I was going to and how the people there acted regarding my case. We also talked about prayer.

My sons and I always ended our visits with a prayer. Jeanie, too, would bow her head and join us in a listening role. She said once that she was so impressed with my sons and how they believed everything would work out with God's help. She told me that because of us, she had started praying more.

CHAPTER 10

Having Jeanie in our lives turned out to be a tremendous blessing in court. I had paid her over $3,400 for the right to see my sons. My wife and I both knew something had to be done. This was money that should have been going to raise our sons, not going to an unnecessary observer of our lives.

My wife's attorney and my attorney got together and scheduled a court date to detail visitation on the pending divorce, with the dual purpose of getting DCFS off my back. Since you can't go to court for that, the two attorneys devised a plan.

They subpoenaed three people to court for this hearing. They called for Detective Welker, Jeanie, and Angie, Jeanie's supervisor at DCFS. The morning of the court date began with a bang, thanks to Angie.

Everyone had gathered in the hall outside the courtroom, waiting for the judge to call us in. It was apparent the moment Angie arrived that she was not happy. I was standing by one wall as she came around the corner. She walked by me with a scowl and announced, "I don't know why I am even here. I have more important things to do."

Angie then walked over to Detective Welker and gave him a big smile and greeting—not the same attitude she'd shown me.

She leaned in close and whispered to him. The waiting area was not very large, so I did not register her whisperings as anything strange at the time; that is, until she left him, went over to my wife and did the same thing.

She gave my wife the same toothy greeting and the all-business whisper. I waited patiently for my turn, but I was not to be third in line. After that, my wife and Angie went over to Jeanie—smile, greet, whisper. Then Angie headed back over to Detective Welker.

About that time, my lawyer, Howard, walked in. I observed Angie go back and forth among Detective Welker, my wife, and Jeanie one more time. I decided I should tell Howard what she was doing. After all, he might need to prepare for something.

So I leaned in close and quietly said to my 6'2", 230-pound counsel, "Angie is going around whispering something to everybody." In a thunderous booming voice, he looked right at her and said, "I don't care what she is whispering!" With that, the hallway ceased breathing. Everyone looked right at us. I was looking at Howard, and he was looking at Angie.

I tried to salvage something and quietly said, "Don't piss her off." He again responded, looking at her and yelling, "I don't care if I do piss her off. She's an idiot!" And with that, Angie was done whispering, and the doors to the courtroom opened.

My wife, the attorneys, and I walked into the empty courtroom and sat in front. The judge confirmed that we were there to deal with a visitation issue. He also stated that it was unusual to deal with this before the day of the divorce but that we had a problem regarding DCFS that we hoped to resolve. He told us, to my surprise, that DCFS does not have to listen to him, but he would do what he could to help us work this out.

Howard addressed the judge first. He outlined that I had been arrested for possession of child pornography and stated that DCFS had put excessive constraints on me. He told the judge that

CHAPTER 10

when this hearing was over, he hoped the judge would be able to make a solid recommendation to DCFS that would allow me to see my sons without the costly supervision.

The judge asked my wife's attorney, Kent, if he had any opening comments. Kent stood up and stated that his client, my wife, felt the same way I did, that under the circumstances, these constraints were excessive. With that, my attorney called in the first witness.

Detective Welker came through the doors and took the stand. Howard asked the standard questions about his name, title, and duties with the police force, and Detective Welker replied that he was a computer forensic detective. Then my attorney got to the pertinent questions.

Howard asked Detective Welker if he had reviewed all the information linked to my arrest, and Detective Welker affirmed that he had. My attorney then asked if he found anything that would lead him to believe that I had abused any children in any manner. Detective Welker replied that he had not. Then came the main point of the questioning. He asked Detective Welker if he had any evidence that would lead him to believe that my sons were in any danger by spending time with me unsupervised. Detective Welker replied that he had no evidence supporting that I had or would cause any harm to my sons. The detective was dismissed from the stand with no questions from my wife's attorney—me one, DCFS zero.

Howard called Angie as the next witness. She had not heard any of the previous discussions among the judge, the attorneys, and Detective Welker. She took her place on the stand and sat back in the chair as my attorney approached the podium.

Angie reclined and slouched as far as possible in the hard courtroom chair. Her body language revealed what she had announced in the hall—"I don't know why I am even here. I have more important things to do."

Howard recited the same set of standard questions he had asked Detective Welker. He also asked Angie about her position at DCFS and how long she had been there. She replied that she was a supervisor and had been there for four years. Then the fun started.

Howard asked Angie, very pointedly, if she was responsible for making sure I was not able to have contact with my sons unless a DCFS supervisor was in attendance. She replied that she was. My attorney asked her why that was, and she replied that they do so in all these cases. (Actually, they do not.) My attorney then asked her if they treat people who have sexually abused children the same way. She replied that they do because "the cases were the same."

I was ready to jump up from the table, but Howard kept it very cool. I don't know how he managed to keep his voice calm at that moment, but that is why he makes the big money.

Next, Howard asked Angie if she had interviewed my sons, to which she replied that she had. He then asked her if she remembered that meeting. She replied that she did. He followed this up by asking her when that meeting occurred. She replied, "Sometime in June."

I had been arrested in July.

Angie probably did not know that because she had come to the court empty-handed. She brought no paperwork about my case when she walked through the courtroom door.

There was quiet in the courtroom as my attorney looked at the judge. It took a second for the judge to catch this, but then with a curious look, he asked my attorney if he could ask the witness a quick question. With a slight smile, Howard replied, "Of course, Your Honor."

The judge asked Angie if I was under investigation by DCFS before this incident, to which Angie replied, "Yes." Looking surprised, the judge repeated his question, to which Angie replied that no, this was the first incident with me. The judge wanted to

CHAPTER 10

clarify and reiterated that this was the first case she had with me and asked if that was correct. She confirmed it was, and the judge allowed my attorney to move on. Howard decided this would be a good time for my wife's attorney to try his luck with Angie and answered that he had no further questions. Throughout the process, Angie remained slumped in the chair in a careless position. But now, it was the "enemy's" time to ask questions.

The judge called for my wife's attorney to take his turn. I will never forget Angie's reaction. She sat up straight in her chair, smiled, and even flipped her hair out of her face. She communicated that she was ready for this and that it was going to be good. She sat there with a very straight, stiff posture, hands folded in her lap. My wife's attorney, undoubtedly Angie's ally, approached the podium. I am so glad I did not know what was coming.

My wife's attorney, Kent, approached the podium and said, "Mrs. Morgan, you stated that you treat men who have been arrested for possessing child pornography the same as you do men who have sexually abused children. Are there studies out there to back up your position?"

The look on Angie's face was priceless. She had just been blindsided. She let out a puff of air and leaned back in the chair once again. She said, "Well, I am sure there are studies on that." Kent followed that up by asking if she had read any of those studies and if she could share just one of them with the court. Angie replied that she was sure she had read them but could not recall any of them at the moment.

At that point, Kent had no further questions. He had discredited Angie's statement about why DCFS was dealing with me in the way they were. But it was not over. As Kent went to sit down, the judge decided to get a piece of the action.

The judge asked my attorney if he could ask the witness a few more questions before any closing questions we might have. My attorney agreed, and the judge proceeded. The exchange was a cross between comical and sad.

Judge: "Mrs. Morgan, what are your qualifications for your job? Do you have some sort of degree?"

Mrs. Morgan: "I have a bachelor's degree in family counseling."

Judge: "And how long have you worked for DCFS?"

Mrs. Morgan: "Four years."

Judge: "And how much training has DCFS provided for you in dealing with cases like Mr. Brown's?"

Mrs. Morgan: "We have ongoing training."

Judge: "Ongoing training? What does that mean? When was the last time you had training specifically to deal with someone arrested for possessing child pornography?"

Mrs. Morgan: "We have a week-long conference once a year in Chicago."

Judge: "So you go for a week's worth of training on dealing with possession of child pornography?"

Mrs. Morgan: "The conference deals with all parts of our job."

At this point, the judge dropped his pen on his desk, removed his glasses, and stared at Angie.

Judge: "Mrs. Morgan, exactly how much of this conference is devoted to dealing with men with charges like Mr. Brown?"

Mrs. Morgan: "I don't know. A day, maybe half a day."

Judge: (Pause) "So would it be fair to say that the training at your conference, specific to this case, is maybe one day, a few hours before lunch?"

Mrs. Morgan: "Yes."

Judge: "So would it also be fair to say that in four years of employment, DCFS has provided you with just a few hours of training on dealing with men who have been charged with possession of child pornography?"

Mrs. Morgan: "Yes."

CHAPTER 10

Judge: "I have nothing further."

And with that, the judge asked Howard if he had any other questions.

While this was happening, my attorney quietly asked me to write any thoughts I had on a piece of paper. I wrote down that Angie had interviewed my sons and told my wife everything was fine. My attorney stood back up and addressed this with Angie. He again asked Angie if she remembered interviewing my sons, to which she replied that she did. She added that she interviewed one boy and then the other. She did not recall which boy went first.

My attorney asked a few more questions about the interview, to which she replied that the interview process took about an hour. She also recalled telling my wife that everything with my boys was fine. Neither attorney had any further questions. Angie quickly climbed out of her chair and left the courtroom—me two, DCFS zero.

CHAPTER 11

Next to be called to the stand was Jeanie. Howard again began with the standard questions about her name, address, and age. Then he asked Jeanie how long she had worked for DCFS. She replied that she had been with them as a client supervisor for 19 years.

Howard asked her what she had observed while on visits with my sons and me. Jeanie, with a very professional look on her face, told the court about all the activities we had done. She said the one she was most impressed with was when we went to my woodshop and built a doghouse for a friend's dog.

Jeanie outlined how excited the boys were about building the doghouse. She explained how I was teaching them to use the needed tools and ensuring each step was performed safely. They were excited about using the air-driven power nail gun and the electric saws. She also shared how the boys took turns doing each step. But what most impressed her was that they were doing all this work just to turn around and give it away for free. It was a gift for someone else. I sat there and listened to her describe how this was much more than just spending time with my sons. It had impressed her that I was teaching them life-long values.

CHAPTER 11

Howard's following line of questioning resulted in a home run for our side. He asked Jeanie if she had reported the details of our visits to her supervisor, Angie, at DCFS. Jeanie replied that she had tried but that Angie never returned her calls. She said she had left six or seven messages for Angie as soon as she received the subpoena a few weeks earlier. Angie finally returned her numerous calls the night before this court date.

My attorney then asked her what she wanted to report to Angie. Jeanie replied that she had tried to tell Angie the visits were going well, and she did not think we needed continued supervision.

Howard asked Jeanie what it meant financially to her to be able to supervise the three of us on visits. She replied that she had filed for bankruptcy a short time ago, and the extra money was a blessing. She did not know how she would have made it without us.

Finally, Howard asked Jeanie to describe me as a father. Jeanie said she had supervised for a long time and worked with many fathers over the years, but she did not often work with the "cream of the crop." And then she said it. She looked right into the eyes of the judge and said, "I have done this for 19 years, and I have never met a better father than Mr. Brown."

Tears immediately filled my eyes—me three, DCFS zero.

Jeanie was dismissed, and it came time for the fourth and final witness. Howard could not legally call my wife as a witness because we were technically on different sides of this hearing. But my wife's attorney, Kent, had full power to call her as his witness, and he did.

Kent asked her the same few questions to get things started about her name and age. Then he asked her to describe my relationship with the boys. She stated that I have always had a strong relationship with them. She said they loved me very much and wanted to see me every day. Then Kent asked her about the money I was spending to see them, money that was going to a supervisor instead of family bills. She stated the supervision DCFS had placed on our family needed to be removed and had never been required in the first place. With that, Kent sat down.

Next, it was Howard's turn, and he got right to the point. He asked my wife about Angie's interview with my sons. She recalled Angie had met with all three of them in the lobby of DCFS for about five minutes. Angie had told my wife she would need to talk to the boys privately, to which my wife agreed. My wife stated that Angie walked my two sons to another part of the building. My attorney then asked the question that put the nail in the coffin for Angie's testimony.

Howard asked my wife how long Angie had met with the boys. My wife said, "Five minutes, 10 minutes at the most." My attorney said, "Ten minutes? With each boy?" My wife answered, "No, 10 minutes total. Probably not even that long."

There was one more piece of information Howard wanted to drive home. He asked if Angie had said anything to my wife about the meeting. My wife said Angie told her everything was fine with the boys and there was nothing to worry about.

The questioning concluded, and I believed the score was now me four, DCFS zero. The judge would now rule, although we would soon find out that when you are dealing with DCFS, the score is always you zero, DCFS one.

CHAPTER 12

The judge stated that there seemed to be overwhelming evidence that I should be allowed to see my sons without a supervisor. He reasoned that there was no evidence that I posed a danger to my sons. He added that the $3,400 that had been spent already could have been better spent for our family. But he had one significant concern.

The judge affirmed that he had limited power over DCFS. He worried that he could rule today that I did not need a supervisor, and tomorrow a "certain supervisor" from DCFS could swoop in and take my sons to foster care. He said we would be in juvenile court redoing all this two to three days later to get them back. The evidence would play out there the same way it did here. But he wanted to avoid that scenario for the sake of the children. This ordeal had been hard enough on them already. He did not want them to be in foster care even one day when they had two loving parents.

I could not believe what I was hearing. I had always believed that a judge would have ultimate authority in our justice system. To think that a person with a simple college degree could trump the decision of a judge, for whatever reason, was unbelievable to me.

A judge is a master of the law, bound to look at every case without bias. A judge takes it upon himself to make a decision that is best for all parties. But unfortunately, DCFS does not have to respect a judge's ruling if they do not want to. Knowing this, our judge added something to his decision.

He asked for the four of us to go into his chambers and spend 10 minutes coming up with a list of people willing to voluntarily supervise my visits with the boys for the next few weeks. He wanted to give this situation time to play out in case someone at DCFS held a grudge.

My wife and I came up with a short list of people who could hang out with my sons and me during visits. It included my best friend, Mike, a few friends from church, and my elderly mother. We presented this list to the judge, and he was satisfied. He stated that he was ruling that it is not required that I have supervision while visiting with my sons but suggested that I do so whenever possible.

He stated that he would send this ruling to DCFS in hopes they would focus their attention on some children who were not loved as much as ours were. He wished us all well, and we left the courtroom. But the surprises that day were not over.

CHAPTER 13

My wife and I, along with our attorneys, left the courtroom and parted ways. As soon as I got in my truck, I made a few phone calls. The first person I called was Jeanie. I thanked her for what she said and told her about the judge's ruling. Then she asked me a question.

She asked if I saw Angie talking to her before court and if my wife told me what she said. I told her I had no idea. My wife and I had not had a chance to discuss it. Jeanie said Angie told her she had received a report that I was seen coming out of McDonald's unsupervised with my sons the day before. Angie was going to bring this up to the judge and make sure I received a warning that the next time I did that, she was putting the children in foster care.

Jeanie had told Angie there was no way that happened. She told Angie we were on a visit with her that day, and she was with us the entire time. Jeanie advised Angie that she liked to give us a little space and did not always walk right next to us, but we were never out of her sight.

It took me a second to remember back to the previous day. But then I reminded Jeanie, "We were not at McDonald's yesterday. We went to Dairy Queen. And we used the drive-through because the boys wanted to kick the soccer ball around at my place. We didn't walk in or out of the restaurant."

Jeanie was upset. She confirmed that my account was correct. Then she had a few choice words about Angie and her little scheme to try to get me in trouble with the judge. I let her blow off a little steam before I thanked her again.

Jeanie then told me that she was really going to miss the boys and me. She said the money I paid her for supervising was nice, but for some time now she had felt bad for taking it because she felt like my sons were like her grandkids. Jeanie wished me well and stated again that I was the best father she had ever met. She wanted us to call her sometime so she could see the boys—at no charge.

I thanked her again and told her I would be in touch. The boys and I saw her a few times again. Nothing was arranged; we just bumped into her at McDonald's or Walmart.

I laughed once when I saw her throw down a cigarette in a parking lot and stomp on it to make sure it was gone forever. She had just seen the boys walking toward her. My youngest son also saw it and reminded her that smoking was bad for her.

Most of my contact with Jeanie was by phone. She called me every month or so if I had not called her with an update. When I called to ask her to write a letter to the judge, she responded with a very touching account of what she had observed.

Jeanie and I corresponded by letter every month for several years after that. She once offered to write a poem that I could give to my boys. I agreed, and when her poem arrived, it brought tears to my eyes. It had all the emotion that Jeanie had felt through me during my long legal process.

At some point, Jeanie and I lost contact for about six months. Then a letter from her showed up. She told me things were not

CHAPTER 13

going well for her. She had some medical issues and was in a relationship that she described as physically abusive. She was in the process of moving away from him.

I wrote her back sometime later. As I pen this chapter, I have not heard back from her. I do not know what happened to her, but I hope to find out someday. I pray she is in good health, and I would love for her to see how the boys have grown.

If something has happened to her and she is no longer with us, I hope people will remember her as a responsible, caring individual who fought against the system she worked for so a father could spend more time with the boys he loves.

Thank you, Jeanie.

CHAPTER 14

My experience with the federal court was an amazing thing to behold. It started one morning just before 6:00 a.m. I was living in my best friend Mike's furnished basement where I had moved when my wife and sons came back from Louisiana. I was sound asleep when I heard what sounded like someone trying to break into the front door upstairs. The doorbell rang repeatedly, and the pounding on the front door was relentless and loud. I threw on a shirt and ran up the stairs. As I rounded the corner, I saw two large men standing outside, looking in the sidelight windows of the front door. It was not until I opened the door that I realized I knew one of them.

The imposing, muscular, black man was Loren, the parent of one of the girls I had coached in volleyball for the past three years. He was dressed in all blue with a badge sewn onto his shirt. An equally sizable white man accompanied him. Both were wearing short-sleeved shirts that I believe were worn to intimidate whoever they had to deal with each day.

Loren said, "Hey, Scott, you have been summoned to federal court, and you have to come with us." I asked him if I could put on some street clothes, and he said I could. He walked with me down the stairs and allowed me to get dressed. I believe the other

CHAPTER 14

guy stayed upstairs to secure the perimeter in case six or eight of my friends rushed the house to free me. I have no doubt he would have singlehandedly subdued any number of my friends.

I got in the front seat of an unmarked car with Loren, and his co-agent followed in a similar vehicle. Loren explained that they had arrived in the neighborhood an hour earlier. They knew Mike would be leaving for work early. They waited ten minutes after my friend left his house to make sure he was not returning. Then they came for me. That was fascinating to me. I felt like a dangerous criminal.

While we rode in the car, Loren allowed me to make some phone calls. I began by calling my wife and explaining that the federal court had picked up my case. Neither of us knew why, but she was going to try to find out what was happening.

I called my lawyer, Howard, who was unaware that this was happening. It appears that when the feds start moving, everything is a surprise. He told me to come and see him at his office as soon as I got released.

I called Mike who was just arriving at work. I explained to him there was nothing he could do right then and that I would call him when I knew something.

Loren gave me the basics. He was a city police officer but doubled as a federal agent when they called on him. He saw the assignment come across the day before and asked to be assigned to it. Loren said he was taking me to the city police station where we would pick up the arresting officer, Detective Welker.

He also explained that the federal court does not have a large case load like the state courts and that when we arrived in Champaign, 45 minutes away, I would be one of the few cases they would have that day.

Loren answered my questions very respectfully, but he was short and to the point, consistent with his "parent personality" at our games. Most parents came up and talked to me at some point during the season. But although Loren came to most of his daughter's games, he never talked to me. He always sat next to his wife or stood by the door when he was hired for security. I walked past him a few times and said hi, but it was always clear that he did not want to talk to me. His massive size was intimidating.

I always treated his daughter fairly, and she was one of the stars of our team every year. She was athletic and brilliant, and hardly ever sat on the bench. I rarely raised my voice when coaching, never wanting to humiliate the players. I was convinced Loren was not a fan of mine for some reason. And now, he was the one in charge of transporting me to federal court.

A few minutes after entering the local police station, I realized I might have misjudged Loren. I was in the same interrogation room as before and was waiting for something to happen. I tried to reach my wife on my cell phone, but I could not get a signal in the large block building. Loren poked his head in to see if I needed anything. I explained my phone problems to him. He stepped into the room, handed me his cell phone, and said, "Try mine. It should work in here." Then he stepped back out and shut the door.

I was shocked. It was an unexpected kind gesture.

I called my wife and talked to her for a few minutes before the door flew open. There stood Todd, the assistant chief of police and one of my neighbors. He looked angry. There was a camera on the ceiling of the little room. He must have noticed in his interrogation room that I was on the phone without his permission, and he intended to correct this.

Todd told me to hang up. He then took the phone from me and asked whose phone it was. I said that Loren let me use it because I was not getting reception on mine. At that moment, Loren came to the door and took the phone from him. They stepped into the hall outside the door. I could hear a raised voice, and I knew it was

CHAPTER 14

not Loren's. He was getting an earful from my neighbor Todd. I realized that what Loren had done to help me out may have been against policy.

I sat alone in the little room for another 10 minutes. Eventually, Todd came in with Detective Welker. They had me empty my pockets and then tossed my possessions in a brown grocery bag. They logged the contents on a piece of paper that I signed. Detective Welker told me it was time to go. We walked out into the hall and were joined by Loren. He did not look like he was upset from the reprimand he had received from his boss.

We were preparing to go to the parking lot when Detective Welker told me he would put me in shackles for the trip to Champaign. He handcuffed my hands in front of me and put another set around both of my ankles. When I took a step forward, I told him that the ankle shackles were too tight and that they were hurting. He instructed me just to walk more slowly.

This was going to be a long 45-minute ride.

I shuffled across the parking garage to the unmarked car. As I reached the passenger door, Detective Welker opened it and told me to get in. Loren, however, told me to wait a minute. He knelt on one knee and loosened my ankle shackles. He asked me if that was better, and I said that it was. He then loosened my handcuffs a little. I did not realize how tight they were until I had a little room to wiggle in them. The whole time this was happening, Detective Welker sat in the driver's seat, eyes forward, car running. He was anxious to go. I climbed into the front seat, and Loren sat in the back. I was glad Loren was going to be there for the trip.

CHAPTER 15

The ride to federal court was uneventful. I asked Detective Welker a few questions about why this was happening. His replies were always dramatic. He said the feds heard what I had done, and the grand jury chose to indict me. It would be up to the judge if I would be released or not while awaiting trial. I asked him if all cases like mine went federal. He replied that they did not. I asked him why mine was. He replied it was because mine was a serious case.

I remember my next thought. Serious? Really? I repeated what I had told him in the interrogation room. I was curious if the federal grand jury knew the facts of what happened. Did they know the facts of the case? Detective Welker did not reply. He just drove ahead. In line with his personality, Loren said nothing the entire trip there.

We arrived at the federal courthouse in just under an hour. We went through a security gate and circled down under the building to a small parking area that only fit three cars. We walked the short distance to the entrance door, and someone buzzed us in. As we entered the room, I saw a woman standing with her back to us, typing on a computer. Noticing a scale to record weight, a tape measure on the wall for height, and a camera for mug shots, I

CHAPTER 15

realized we were in a processing area. The woman went about her business, turned around, and did a double take at me. She then looked at Detective Welker and in an incredulous voice said, "Take him out of the cuffs. He is getting ready to go in front of the judge!"

It was interesting how she said those words. I can only guess that either this was one of Detective Welker's first trips to federal court or he had left me in cuffs because my case was "serious."

The way she reprimanded Detective Welker stuck with me. It was like a mother telling her son not to walk on the new carpet wearing his outside shoes. He knows better, but he is doing it anyway.

After a few minutes, the woman in processing walked me to a chair behind a glass wall. A young woman stepped in, sat across from me behind the glass, and told me she was Mrs. White from probation. She needed to ask me some questions.

She wanted to know if I had been depressed since finding out that I was being charged in federal court. I explained to her that obviously these last few months had been depressing. Then she asked the main question. At any time had I considered suicide since getting charged?

It took me no time to answer. I explained that I had two sons at home whom I loved very much, and I would never consider suicide. I thought my answer was sufficient to convince her.

Next, she asked me for my lawyer's name and phone number. She said she needed to call him and would return shortly. Upon returning, she informed me that my lawyer agreed that it was highly unlikely I would try to commit suicide. He confirmed that I had a strong relationship with my sons. She then told me that I would appear before the judge, and it would be up to him if I would be released or taken into custody.

My stress level skyrocketed. The only that went through my mind was if I would see my sons that evening. It was a visitation day, and I was scheduled to pick them up after school. I didn't have any specific plans, but we would have fun whatever we did.

I had not seen them in two days. If I could not see them, who would spend time with them? Being taken into custody would not benefit my sons or me. The last thing I told Mrs. White was how much I hoped to go home because tonight was a visitation night, and my sons were expecting me.

At some point, Detective Welker and I walked to the federal courtroom. I was in awe. It was not a standard state courtroom, and I can't adequately describe its majesty.

Everything was trimmed in dark, expensive-looking wood. Cleanliness was in the air. This courtroom looked like it was built for a movie set. The carpet appeared new and just vacuumed. The judge's desk was the centerpiece of the room. It was large and sat much higher than in a state court. Next to it, the court reporter had a spotless area equipped with a computer. The room's ceiling was so high that it looked like a perfect place to host a small concert.

In state court, you might have 30 people waiting their turn in front of the judge. Each of them may have supporters there watching the proceedings. Every day, all those hands and shoes would make it impossible to keep the place looking as pristine as this federal court.

At state court, the lawyers would all be standing around waiting for their turn to go before the judge. Sometimes they would ask for a few more minutes while waiting for their client to appear. State court is often controlled chaos, but not federal court.

The judge, court reporter, Detective Welker, Loren, Mrs. White, an older gentleman in uniform who appeared to be there for security, and I were the only ones occupying the massive room. The time was set aside solely for me. Again, I started to feel like I was in some real trouble. But the thought kept going through my mind on replay. Would I be able to see my sons that night?

CHAPTER 15

The proceedings of that court were not like state court. This was not a 30-second, set bail, and leave hearing. The judge started by stating why I was there. The grand jury had looked at the evidence provided by the federal agent, Detective Welker, and found enough cause to charge me. After a few minutes, he got to probation and stated they did not find a reason to take me into custody. Thank God! I was going to see my sons tonight.

Then the judge read a long list of conditions I would have to follow after I left court. I was not to partake in any illegal drugs and was not to use excessive alcohol. Those two I was already following. I had not smoked marijuana in the past 14 years, ever since I had been married. And before that, it was only once every few months or so. I had never used any other illegal drugs in my entire life.

After my arrest, I stopped drinking alcohol. I was never a heavy drinker and had always kept it to beer. I knew alcohol makes people more emotional, and I didn't need anything to add to my already fragile emotions.

Next, the judge stated that I was not to receive any "sexually arousing material" via the Internet or in print. He said that if I had a computer, I would have to have it monitored by probation. Detective Welker had confiscated my computer, and I had not obtained a new one. I wanted to get one because I had sold some items on eBay and needed to get caught up.

The judge dismissed me and told me I needed to go to the probation office immediately. I was free to go after that. I went to probation and met with Mrs. White. She was young but very in charge, someone who would not take any crap. She went through the rules the judge had laid out. I signed a few forms showing that I agreed. Then Mrs. White asked me where I was currently living.

I explained I had moved into my best friend Mike's basement. She said she would contact him immediately to set up a time to visit his house. She also let me know that she would be searching his entire house, and she would do this often with no warning.

I knew Mike would have trouble agreeing to that. There was nothing illegal in his house, and he did not partake in any illegal activities, but he was a private person. He would see these periodic searches as an invasion of his privacy. Mrs. White saw the concern on my face and asked if I had anyone else I could live with if he did not agree to these surprise searches of his residence. I immediately knew then that I would be moving back home to my elderly mother's house.

After my meeting with Mrs. White, I had to make one more stop in processing. The same woman was there and told me she would need some information since I had been formally charged and that she would be with me shortly. A few minutes later, Detective Welker popped his head into the room. He asked the woman how much longer I would be because he had to return to Decatur. He stated that if it took a while, he would leave without me.

After thinking about that for a moment, I asked the woman how I was supposed to get home if the detective left. She said it was up to me and that some people call a cab, walk, or have someone pick them up. When she was finished, I would be walked to the front door and released. I would be free to go whether I had a way home or not.

I was sitting in my assigned chair when Loren walked in. He sat next to me and asked if I was okay. I said yes but that I was wondering how to get home if he and Detective Welker left. The woman had still not started my processing, so I asked Loren how much longer they would be able to wait. I was relieved when he said they would take me back to Decatur.

Five minutes later, Detective Welker walked back into the room. He asked the woman how much longer it would be, and she

CHAPTER 15

replied that she did not know. He thundered, "I am ready to go," and walked out of the room. Loren did not move.

I wasn't sure what would happen if Detective Welker left, and Loren was still sitting in the chair next to me. Detective Welker didn't go but returned about five minutes later. I can only imagine that when he left, he assumed Loren would soon follow. Loren was still sitting next to me.

Detective Welker looked at me like I had something to do with the wait. I was more than ready to forget the whole thing and leave. He told Loren, "I have to go." After a three-second pause, Loren stood up and walked to the door. Then they both walked out of the room.

I started thinking about my options. A cab ride would be expensive; walking was out of the question; a rental car would be pricy. The only thing I could do was call some of my friends until I found one willing to drive almost an hour to pick me up and then take me back home. As I was planning my next move, Loren walked back into the room. He sat beside me and calmly said, "We're going to wait."

CHAPTER 16

It took another 20 minutes before processing was done. Loren patiently sat in his chair next to mine. Detective Welker occasionally looked through the window in the door, but he did not come back into the room. Loren and I stood up when the woman in charge announced we were done, and I was free to go. I followed Loren out of the room.

Detective Welker was standing just outside the door, waiting impatiently. As soon as he saw us coming, he moved into a speed walk straight for the exit door. He beat us to the car and had it running before Loren, and I got out of the building.

I sat in the front seat like before, but I was not wearing shackles this time. As we pulled out of the federal parking lot, Loren offered me my cell phone that was in the brown bag on the back seat. I called my wife. She had received some information from a neighbor about this trip to federal court. I learned that many more people knew about it than I first realized.

Our neighbor found out the previous night that I would be picked up. When she was out working in her yard, two women walked up with the daily gossip. Both of their husbands were Decatur police detectives and wondered if our neighbor had heard the "good news."

CHAPTER 16

They told her I would be taken to federal court in the morning. They also said their husbands were excited because going to federal court meant I would get more years in jail. My wife was in tears when she relayed this information to me.

She asked me what exactly "more years in jail" meant, but I had no idea. I shared the events of the day, and she wondered what would happen to my sons if I went away to prison. I had no answer.

After hanging up the phone, several thoughts crossed my mind. What did the police know that I did not? Why did they believe that federal court meant more years in jail? Why did the federal court pick up my case anyway? What was going to happen to my sons if I went away to prison?

I knew I was in trouble, but surely my actions were not something that would take me away from raising my sons. One question from the gossip irritated me more than all the others. How could the detectives' wives comment that the police were excited because this meant more years in prison?

Did they not think of my sons at all? Do they not understand how many children in America grow up without a dad? Do they have any idea of what actually happened in my case?

They should have been sad thinking about my two wonderful boys growing up without their father. They should have realized the sorrow my sons would go through. They should have had compassion for my sons.

CHAPTER 17

After I hung up the phone, I sat quietly for a while. At some point on the trip, I realized I needed to get my truck at my best friend's house. I asked Detective Welker if he could drop me off where they had picked me up that morning. It was only two blocks off the highway we were traveling on. Detective Welker continued his hostile attitude toward me.

He replied that he was not departing from his course from the federal courthouse to the police department. I asked how I was supposed to get my truck. Dramatically, he took his foot off the gas and started to slow down. We had been traveling just over 65 miles per hour on the highway. He looked over at me and said, "I can pull over and let you out right here if you want, and you can walk home."

I quickly said it was too far to walk (we were still 35 miles from Decatur) and asked if he could drop me off at the stoplight after we got off the highway. He let me know that was only an option if the stoplight was red and he had to come to a stop. I was getting nowhere with him.

I told him there was a chance that the light at the big intersection where Walmart was located would be red. If it was not, I asked if he could just pull off to the side and let me out there.

CHAPTER 17

I would walk across the intersection to a Walgreens and have my friend pick me up there. He said that was fine but that when he pulled over, I had to get out quickly because he needed to get back to the station. Finally we had an agreement.

I called my best friend, Mike, and asked him to pick me up in the Walgreens parking lot. I did not give him any details but told him I would inform him about it when we met. We were about half a mile from the large intersection when Loren spoke his first words in 30 minutes.

We were in the right lane, coming up on the stoplight. Loren said, "We will drop you off in the Walgreens parking lot, so you don't have to cross the intersection on foot."

I glanced over at Detective Welker who glanced back at Loren in the mirror. Within seconds we veered into the left lane preparing for the turn into Walgreens. We turned the corner and pulled onto the little turn ramp on the edge of the Walgreens property. Just as the car's back wheels got on the lot, we stopped, as far away from the store as possible. Detective Welker was making a statement.

As I exited the car, I looked into the back seat and saw Loren looking at me. I thanked him for everything, and he said, "Good luck." I closed the door. That was the last time I saw him.

A few months later, I saw Loren's wife at Walmart. She smiled as soon as she saw me, and I walked over to her. She asked me how I was doing, and I briefly filled her in on the case. I asked her to pass along my appreciation to Loren. I told her the trip to federal court would not have been the same without him. I explained to her about the cell phone and the tight shackles. I told her that her husband had stuck up for me when Detective Welker wanted to drop me off 45 minutes from home. And then I asked her a question.

I knew they were a Christian family, and I asked her how Loren could keep his Christian values when all he saw every day were people accused of doing wrong. His job put him around the worst of the worst every day. I wanted to know how he kept his faith in humans.

She told me that his faith was in God, not humans, and that it was not easy for him. He is one of the few true Christians in the department and is as strong spiritually as he is physically. I could not imagine how he handled it. His wife said he prays daily and does not let others negatively influence his life. He knows that we all sin, and he does his best not to judge anyone.

She finished by sharing that even though Loren had not talked to me much at the games, he genuinely liked how I coached his daughter. I appreciated that. I shook her hand and reminded her again to thank him for me. I am sure she did. I left Walmart, fighting back tears.

Someday I hope to have a quick conversation with Loren. He is a man of few words, so I am sure I will do most of the talking.

Reflection Section for Chapters 8-17 available on page 215

CHAPTER 18

One of the first things I did upon my return from federal court was go see my lawyer, Howard. I had met him 15 years earlier at church. Howard and I had played softball together all those years, often going out to various watering holes after the games. We also golfed together in the annual church outing, and I considered us friends.

I chose him as my lawyer the night I was arrested. Before the police put me in the car, I asked my wife to call him. Howard was available the next day when I got out of jail. Later, he had done a terrific job when we wanted DCFS to remove the supervisor requirement for when I spent time with my children. He also did a great job explaining what was happening as I was dealing with charges in state court. But this was now a federal case, and things were changing fast.

When I met with Howard after my first appearance in federal court, he filled me in on the good and the bad. He noted on the positive side that this would now be a fair fight. He told me that the state prosecutor assigned to my case was a vindictive person regarding these cases. She would have pulled out all the stops to charge me with as many things as possible.

She would do no less than paint me as the worst creature on the face of the earth. However, Howard still felt that the details of my case would result in my getting probation in the state, which was good, and because the federal court had picked up my case, the state court would likely drop the charges.

Federal, he explained, was a different story. They would only charge me with what they felt I was guilty of. They would not tack on the other charges that the state court would, which was good. But the federal prosecutors had a conviction rate of over 98 percent. He believed my crime would carry a five-year mandatory prison sentence, which was very bad.

That did not sound like a fair fight to me. I once again sat in disbelief that I could be taken from my sons for five years. They were eight and 11 at that time. They would be at least 13 and 16 when I could see them again. I would miss so much of their lives.

I asked Howard if there was any chance that we could get a not guilty verdict. He said the main problem with that was that I had already admitted to Detective Welker that I had seen the illegal videos come on my computer. And even though I did not watch them and attempted to delete them, they were still on my computer. In the eyes of the court, that meant I was guilty of possession. He then reminded me to never talk to a detective without my lawyer present. I assured him that it would never happen again.

A month later, Howard and I had to appear before the federal judge to hear the charges and enter my not guilty plea. We did this to buy some time. I remember watching my lawyer during these proceedings and thinking he did not look like the same man who spoke confidently to the state judge. He was not the same man who had orchestrated getting Angie and DCFS out of my life. He looked like a small fish in a large pond. He was not a man who talked to the judge with confidence.

CHAPTER 18

I could tell immediately that the judge and the federal prosecutor knew each other well. Before the proceedings started, they were laughing about the last college basketball game they had seen. My lawyer, on the other hand, was not part of this fraternal exchange. I suspected that he was not the right man for this job.

At federal court that day, I was charged with possession of child pornography. I saw the big difference between state court and federal court that Howard had mentioned. State prosecutors charge you for as much as they can and then whittle down to what they think they can get a conviction for. Federal court is the opposite. Federal prosecutors charge you with precisely what you did. With a 98 percent conviction rate, they don't need to pile on extras, and there will be no bargaining. I later learned that if you do not take their first deal, the deals will get worse.

A few days after my not guilty plea in front of the federal judge, I received support for my suspicions about Howard not being the right man for this job. A respected member of my church came to me and asked if I had thought of getting a different lawyer now that this was a federal case. His concern was that even though Howard was known to do well in state court, he did not have any federal experience. I told this person that I already had those same thoughts.

I decided to see if there was someone else out there who could help me. I reflected on one of my favorite television shows—*Boston Legal*—a show starring William Shatner as lawyer Denny Crain and James Spader as lawyer Allen Shore. Week after week, Allen Shore was presented with an unwinnable legal case. Week after week, he successfully won the case for his client. In the courtroom, Allen Shore was "the Man." What I needed was "the Man."

After my arrest, I stopped going to my 1,200-member church. I started attending a 16-member house church run by Troy, one of my large church's associate pastors. It was a friendly little group that I became very close to. They sincerely cared for my sons and me.

I decided to look for another lawyer. The following Sunday, I asked Brian, a lawyer and one of the men at the house church, if he knew a federal attorney who could help me. I told him I felt there was probably one lawyer out there who could help me at this point—and he had to be "the Man."

Brian said he would contact a few of his old college buddies who were lawyers in Champaign and ask around. He promised to get back to me that week.

On Tuesday, Brian called with what would turn out to be the single most helpful call in my search for legal counsel. Brian said that something incredible had happened. He said he called two of his college buddies who, incidentally, did not know each other. He gave each of them a brief description of my case and asked if they knew someone who could help. Both his friends mentioned the same name—Steve Beckett.

Steve was a semi-retired lawyer who spent his time as a teacher at the University of Illinois College of Law. He had worked in the federal court system for over 20 years. Brian told me that both his buddies considered Steve "the Man."

My call to Steve's office did not start well. When I told the secretary the reason for my call, she informed me that Steve only took one or two cases a year due to his commitment to teaching and was not taking new ones. However, she let me know that there was another lawyer in their firm who handled these cases in federal court.

I told her that my case had some circumstances that were not normal in these cases. I needed an attorney who could relate this to the prosecutor and judge in federal court. And yes, I told her that I felt there was probably only one person out there who could help me, and that Steve was recommended as that person—the Man.

CHAPTER 18

She put me on hold for the longest two minutes of my life. When she returned, she told me that Steve's personal secretary would email him the details and that she would call me later that day. I thanked her and hung up the phone.

Later that day, I received a call. The secretary asked me if I would be able to meet Steve in his office at 8:00 a.m. that coming Friday. I confirmed that I could. I would have met him anytime on any day, anywhere I could.

On Friday morning at 7:30, I arrived at Steve's office, which was 45 minutes from my house. I was feeling very anxious. Questions were darting through my mind as I sat in the quiet of my truck. Would he be able to help me? I had prayed many times that week, asking God that Steve would agree to take my case. I had also asked a few house church members to pray that Steve would take my case.

Would Steve be able to get me out of this five-year mandatory minimum prison sentence I had heard about from Howard? I had spent time on my new computer looking at other cases. Sure enough, others had received this five-year prison sentence from federal judges. As 8:00 a.m. closed in, it was time to go meet "the Man."

Steve and I talked for over an hour in his office. I detailed everything that had happened. During some of the account, I could not hold back the tears. Steve seemed very caring. He did not appear to be in a hurry and was good about keeping me on track about the facts.

At the beginning of the meeting, I gave him copies of the paperwork I had received from state and federal courts. He flipped through the pages and asked me several questions. I do not remember all of them, but I do remember one. He wanted me to explain how child pornography came onto my computer when I had requested adult pornography.

CHAPTER 19

In Steve's office that early Friday morning, I told him that the program I was using to download pornography was LimeWire. He said he was familiar with that program because there are thousands of men in prison right now for receiving child pornography after using that program. That did not make me feel any better.

I told him that I learned over time that the names of the videos did not always tell you what was on them. I explained that I most commonly searched for videos using the search term "new porn." I told him that as the videos were coming onto the computer, I could preview maybe half of them. The others I had to let finish downloading to see what they were. If I could preview a video I did not want, I would stop the download.

For videos that did not allow previews, I would let it finish downloading and check them out later. The downloads would remain on the LimeWire screen as long as I left the computer running. I would then click on the newly downloaded videos to see what they were. If they were anything I did not want, including child pornography, I would hit the "X" button to delete them. But I also told him that I had learned that action did not delete the videos from my computer.

CHAPTER 19

I also gave Steve a specific example of at least one time when that happened. I was looking at a website that allowed various videos to be sent. I found a fantastic video of a young boy about nine or 10 years old who was a master of the video game *Guitar Hero*. In that video, the kid played the most challenging song on the most difficult level on the guitar-styled game controller.

I had never seen anyone move their hands that fast on a real or a fake guitar. At that time, my oldest son and I played that game daily. I knew he would want to see this video. I called him to the computer, and we both watched in amazement. After watching the video, my son ran to our Xbox game system to practice. I went to LimeWire. I wanted to see if there were more videos out there like that one.

I typed in something like "9-year-old guitar hero." That title was too long and specific because it only resulted in a few videos. I clicked on them and saw the same video my son and I had just watched. I shortened my search parameters and let LimeWire bring me the videos.

I searched for things like "9 guitar" and "9-year-old guitar." I then shortened my search to "9yo guitar" and eventually "9yo." As I abbreviated the search title, more and more possible videos came up. Later, when I went through the videos I had downloaded, I found a few more videos of this amazing gamer. But there were also child pornography videos that had come through.

I explained to Steve that I would click on these new videos, and if there was one of the young *Guitar Hero* master, I would write down the exact name of the video. I then searched for that video on my computer and showed it to my son. I also found some other videos that were either incredible, funny, or interesting things that nine-year-old kids do. My son and I enjoyed watching those too. Steve asked me what I did if I realized the video was one of the illegal ones that had caused my arrest. I told him I hit the "X" button on the video player and thought that took care of it.

After meeting with me for over an hour, Steve decided to take my case. But the next thing he said was not what I wanted to hear. He informed me that more than likely, I would have to plead guilty to possession.

CHAPTER 20

Steve was the second attorney to remind me that I had admitted to the detective that I had seen these illegal videos on my computer screen up to five years earlier and continued the same action that brought them in repeatedly. That pretty much took care of any chance of pleading not guilty.

I was disappointed with this recommendation and asked Steve about the fact that I did not watch those videos and thought I deleted them as soon as they came through. Then Steve gave me a lesson from his experience.

He once had a client who tried to argue against possession in front of the judge. After admitting to the detectives that he had downloaded those videos, he later changed his story, entering a plea of not guilty. The guy came up with stories that involved not knowing how the videos got on his computer. He told the judge and jury that the computer was in a public area of his house. There was no telling who in his family might have downloaded them. Maybe it was his wife, or perhaps it was his young children. He told the judge there was no way they could pin it all on him. Steve then said, "The judge was not amused."

Make a note. This guy found out that it is not a good idea to try to lie in federal court. The judge gave him a sentence of nearly 10 years in federal prison. His young children would be adults the next time he could spend real time with them. I did not want to take that chance.

Drawing from his years of experience, Steve told me what would happen if I plead not guilty. He said it would be an effortless day for the prosecutor. He described how the prosecutor would get up in front of the jury and tell them that the government is not challenging how the videos got to my computer. He may even inform the jury that they are not challenging whether I have led an honest life. He would not question that I have helped many kids in my years of teaching and coaching. He would probably agree with everything my attorney said about my life of helping others. And then he would drop the bomb.

The prosecutor would show the jury in court on a big screen a few of the most disgusting videos he could find on my computer. He would explain that the detectives found those videos on my computer. He would explain that I admitted to downloading these types of videos. He would then tell the jury that he was only asking them if I had possession of these videos on my computer. After seeing the video clips, the jury would be sickened and find me guilty of possession. But there was more.

As of right then, the prosecutor was only charging me with possession. If I plead not guilty, he would enhance the charges. Remember when I said the best deal in federal court was your first offer? Enhancing the charges is common in federal court if you do not take their first offer.

If I plead not guilty and took my case to trial, the prosecutor would also charge me with distribution. LimeWire is a file-sharing program. Just as my computer searched other computers and copied the videos from them, other computers could get

CHAPTER 20

these videos from my computer. Therefore, I was responsible for distributing and trading illegal videos. This minor enhancement could give me more than 10 years in prison instead of five.

If I were to plead not guilty, I would be telling the judge that the prosecutors have it all wrong. But when the evidence was presented and the verdict came in from the jury, it would be clear that I had wasted the court's time. This scenario would not please a federal judge.

Even though I was disappointed by this information, I believed Steve was right. My concern turned to the five-year mandatory minimum prison sentence that Howard had explained. I asked Steve if this was correct, and he gave me the best news of the day.

Steve said he was not positive, but he believed if the prosecutor only charged me with possession, the five-year mandatory minimum did not apply. He would call the prosecutor later that day and find out. He told me that the sentence could be as much as 10 years, but he believed I was also eligible for probation.

Hearing that I might be eligible for probation was the best news I had heard in months. My first meeting with Steve was over, and I was satisfied that he was taking my case.

I remember walking back to my truck as I left his office. I closed the door, sat behind the wheel, and cried for a short time. I also prayed.

I thanked God that probation was possible, although I ignored that Steve only said he would check to see. I believed things had turned around. I immediately got on the phone and passed on the information about the meeting to my wife, my best friend Mike, my brothers, friends at my house church, and anyone else who answered their phone. I was on the phone the entire 45-minute trip home.

I explained to everyone I spoke with that I would likely have to plead guilty and that it could result in up to 10 years in prison.

But I also told them there might not be a five-year mandatory minimum and that, more importantly, I might be eligible for probation. I would find out a day later from Steve.

The following day I was building a shed with Guy, one of my friends from church. I had just walked to my truck to get some more lumber when my phone rang. It was Steve. I can still hear his words. "Hi, Scott. This is Steve. How would you like some good news for a change?"

Steve explained that he talked to the prosecutor and that I was only being charged with possession. This charge had no five-year mandatory minimum. The range was probation up to 10 years in prison.

After this short but significant information, I thanked Steve and agreed to talk in a few days. I sat in the back of my truck with tears in my eyes. My friend Guy came over and asked if everything was okay. I told him about the call. With a big smile he said, "Prayer works."

He told me that he, along with other house church members, had been praying for the possibility of probation. They were also praying that the five-year mandatory minimum would not apply. He told me God was watching over this situation and that if I trusted Him, everything would work out for His glory. I told Guy that I couldn't imagine that God would want me in prison helping prisoners rather than raising my sons.

CHAPTER 21

Steve and I talked every week while I was waiting for the process of federal justice to be completed. Months had gone by since the first time I had stepped into Steve's office. I found that things do not move quickly in a federal case. We went back to court two or three times for continuances. There were a few months between each of those appearances. It always came down to the schedule. The judge, the prosecutor, and the attorney had to make sure their calendars were clear.

There were further delays. When Steve received the report called discovery from the government, it did not contain the truth. And let me assure you that even in a case where you plead guilty, you want to make sure the judge receives the correct set of facts.

Steve called me one day and asked if I had received a copy of Detective Welker's report. I had not, so Steve told me he would fax it to me immediately. It seems there were a few issues that had to be resolved before I should plead guilty.

The way it works is the arresting detective comes up with his sworn affidavit and presents it to the prosecutor. A copy is also given to the defendant. This sworn affidavit is supposed to be the actual findings in the case. It is to be the government's position on exactly what happened. In many cases, the government's and the defendant's positions are not the same. But as Steve explained, in my case where I was going to plead guilty, the facts should be very close. That was the problem. Detective Welker seemed to have a few things in his sworn affidavit to the court that did not match what we considered the facts.

The first issue we had to deal with was Detective Welker's account of the interview he conducted with me the night of the arrest. Here were his main points. I told him I had been downloading adult pornography for about five years. I had seen some child pornography come through but thought I had deleted them as soon as they popped up. He asked me how many videos were on my computer. When I told him I requested between 25 and 50 by quickly clicking on the titles, he said he had found over 400 videos on my computer. He asked how many of them I thought were child pornography. I had no idea how many there were. That is a summary of the actual interview. However, Detective Welker's account in his sworn affidavit was slightly different.

After Steve faxed the report to me, I saw the differences. Detective Welker's one-sentence summary of that interview said, "Mr. Brown admitted to downloading child pornography for approximately five years and estimates his collection of child pornography videos to be about 50."

I was furious. I immediately called Steve. I told him that was not an accurate account of what I said. He then asked me a crucial question. He wanted to know if I had been advised that the interview was being recorded. I told him it was mentioned to me, but I did not know if it was recorded. Steve said he would contact the police department and get a copy of that interview if it existed. I hoped there was one. If not, it would be my word against the sworn affidavit of a federal detective.

Steve called me a few days later to let me know there was a recording and he had just watched it. He said he would write a

CHAPTER 21

summary of the interview and submit it to the prosecutor. Along with his summary, Steve would send the prosecutor a copy of the interview. He told me not to worry.

The second issue that we had to deal with had two parts. One was more severe than the other. It was in the middle of the forensic part of the extensive report. Steve had read it the day he received the affidavit. I was glad he found it so quickly, which showed he genuinely cared about my case.

The first part of this issue was about the number of illegal videos Detective Welker had discovered. Earlier, in state court, he had reported that forensics had identified 36 illegal videos on my computer and a few images. But now, in this federal report, the number had climbed to 125 illegal videos and four still images. He also claimed that my old hard drive from a few years earlier contained the 125 videos, so even though they were copies, they should be added to the number of illegal videos. I asked Steve if we could get our own forensic person to debate this issue. He told me that was unnecessary.

These videos are not made like old film strips. They are called streaming videos. They are not individual pictures all put together to make a film. Instead, the video flows together regardless of the speed it is recorded. The government decided that since they cannot account for individual images in a streaming video and videos can be made at different recording speeds, they would assign each video a value of 75 images. That means that a two-second streaming video is considered 75 images. So is a 60-minute video.

The federal government also decided that if you have less than three images on your computer, you can turn in your computer to local law enforcement to be destroyed and not face prosecution. An investigation may occur, however.

They also decided that the more images you have, the more severe the penalty will be, but it was capped at 600 images. Once you have 601 images, you are over the maximum, and none of the extras will count any more against you.

At 75 images per video, you hit the 600 mark on your eighth video. Steve explained that since I probably had the original number of 36 illegal videos, it would not make sense to spend over $2,000 for a private forensic scientist to knock the number down from 125. Detective Welker might as well have claimed that all 400 were illegal.

However, Steve felt we did need to address an issue in the second part of the forensic report. Detective Welker had made a finding that directly contradicted what I said had happened. At the end of the report were these words: "Upon further forensic examination, we have determined that Mr. Brown watched many of these videos numerous times."

My first thought was that there was no way that was possible. Detective Welker was not telling the truth and had manipulated the forensic report. I asked Steve what we were going to do.

Steve agreed that we did not want to plead guilty to this account of what happened. He also explained that we did not want to go to the judge and say I had never watched any of these videos when the detective's sworn affidavit said I had. The judge would know one of us was not being truthful. I would not come out on the positive side of that battle. Steve decided right then that he was going to schedule an interview with Detective Welker so we could make sure the two accounts were as close as possible. I could not wait.

CHAPTER 22

A few weeks later, Steve and I met Detective Welker in a conference room at the federal courthouse. We arrived first and waited only a few minutes before Detective Welker walked up. He smiled and said hello to both of us.

This greeting irritated me. Over the previous months, I had come to detest Detective Welker. I had no idea why he had come after me the way he did. I understood that I had broken the law, but there was no excuse for how he was treating me.

He had pulled up to my house with an entourage of seven police cars to make a show to the neighbors. Without justification, he had arranged for DCFS to be involved. On our first trip to federal court, he had no reason to do any of the things he did, and he had no right to treat me like a lesser human being. And now he was lying on his sworn affidavit.

I hated him and had no respect for him. And now, after the way he had mistreated me, he had the nerve to greet me with a hello. At that time, I felt the world would be better if he died.

Detective Welker entered the conference room first. As I started to go in, Steve grabbed my arm, looked at me, and cautioned, "Do not say one word."

Steve is a genius. In our short time together, he knew my personality very well. I am a get-it-done type of person. When I am right, I am also someone who will tell you straight up—no mincing words.

Steve knew I would correct Detective Welker on the spot every time he was in error. He also knew my hatred for Detective Welker. When Steve grabbed my arm and told me not to say a word, it was for my protection. He knew the detective would use anything I said against me. He would find a way. Steve's few words to me were his way of letting me know we were on the same team and "I got this."

Detective Welker sat in a chair at the nearest end of the table and placed a large stack of papers, probably 500 or more, in front of him. I could not believe all that could be connected to my case. Steve sat at the corner of the table's long side, next to Detective Welker but not too close. I sat quietly next to Steve.

Steve began by thanking Detective Welker for coming. He then explained to the detective that his view of how the illegal videos came to my computer and our view—I like to call it the truth—did not match up. Steve told him there were a couple of significant points he would like to see if we could get closer together before both accounts were presented to the judge.

Steve continued by asking Detective Welker if he had a copy of the forensic report with him, which he affirmed. Steve noted that Detective Welker's affidavit stated that Mr. Brown had "moved the illegal videos to new files on his computer." I was not aware of this sentence in the report. Steve must have found that statement after we had talked and before this meeting. Steve asked him to explain what he meant by that statement.

Detective Welker explained that when I requested a video, it came to my computer and went to a temporary file. Once I opened and closed a video by hitting the "X" key on the video player, the video would go to my shared or deleted files.

CHAPTER 22

Steve expressed to Detective Welker that the way the sentence currently read in the report gave the impression that I was intentionally moving those illegal files to other areas on my computer. That would allege that I knew what they were and was possibly trying to save or hide them. Detective Welker agreed that he now saw how that could be a misunderstanding. Steve quickly said we would address that sentence in our report to the prosecutor.

Steve moved to the next issue. He noted that Detective Welker's report stated, "Mr. Brown had watched many of these videos numerous times." He looked at the detective and said, "Can you give me an example of an illegal video that Mr. Brown watched more than once?"

Detective Welker began to flip through his giant stack of papers. He pulled a stack off the top and set them to the side. He had gone to the forensic report for his evidence. When he got about halfway through, he said something like this: "Okay. Right here." He slid this section of his paperwork sideways so he and Steve could see it and then pointed to something on the page. I don't remember the title he referenced, but he said two names, which I'll refer to as Jack and Jill.

Detective Welker said, "Here is a video titled Jack and Jill." He flipped forward five or 10 pages in the report and said, "Here it is again—Jack and Jill." He flipped forward maybe 15 pages and noted that the video was in the report a third time. He then pushed the report the rest of the way toward Steve so he could have a better look. I was tense at that point, but Steve was about to relieve the pressure.

Steve flipped back and forth among the three pages and studied them. After about 20 seconds, he pointed out to the detective that those three videos may have had similar titles but were not the same videos. Steve compared the identifying numbers next to the titles in the forensic report and found they were all different. He then pointed out that they were downloaded at different times. One was from about four years before, and the other two were around a year apart. That did not prove I had watched any one video three times. Steve slid the report back to Detective Welker.

Detective Welker looked at the report and flipped back and forth among the three pages for a few seconds. I do not remember his exact words, but I do remember his reasoning. He claimed that when he saw what he read as the same title three times, he assumed I had watched it three times.

I reflected on Steve's earlier warning—"Do not say one word." I had some things to say, and they would not have been nice. Steve, however, continued to impress me with his words and control. Calmly, he looked at the detective and said, "No problem, just pick any of those three videos and tell us how many times Mr. Brown watched it."

I believe Detective Welker then realized that he was in a corner. In a blink, he said he was unable to do that. He could only identify the first time a video had come on the computer. Steve was ready to move to the next question.

Steve told Detective Welker that my claim was that if I saw an illegal child video come on my screen, I attempted to delete it as soon as I saw what it was. He said the detective's statement that I had watched "many of these videos numerous times" would directly contradict my claim. Steve wanted to know if Detective Welker could tell us exactly how long I had watched any of the videos.

Detective Welker replied that he could only check the last eight or 10 videos that went through the player. I think the number related to the file size. Steve replied that it was fine and asked him to check that section of the report.

CHAPTER 22

Detective Welker flipped to a new section in his towering stack of papers, briefly reviewed some information on one of the pages, and then put down the papers for a final time.

He looked at Steve and said, "None of the last videos that went through the player were watched for more than a few seconds." Steve quickly asked if any of those were child pornography videos. Detective Welker replied that they were.

We learned that one of the last videos to go through the video player was the one Detective Welker was fishing out the night I clicked on it. I looked through my copy of the forensic report later and found that this was a new video I had not previously clicked on. It came on my computer, and I thought I had deleted it within seconds of realizing its content. Obviously, I had not.

After Detective Welker closed his report for the final time, Steve advised that we would be filing our account of what had happened. We would also be challenging some things he had written in his affidavit. The detective acknowledged this, and we all left the room. That was the last time I would ever see Detective Welker.

Steve and I left the federal courthouse and drove the few blocks back to his office. He said he would write our affidavit to submit to the court and include an account of the day's meeting with Detective Welker. He asked if I had any questions. I did—one that had been on my mind for months.

I asked Steve if he now believed my explanation of how all this had happened. Since he was my paid attorney, I thought he would do whatever he could to help me, regardless of his feelings. Attorneys often say their clients lie to them all the time. I wanted to know if Steve was starting to believe me now that we had met with Detective Welker or if he knew I was telling the truth at an earlier time. His reply meant so much to me.

He said he knew I was telling the truth the first time we spoke. He said he had been an attorney for a long time and could tell from the day we met that this was a case of carelessness, not what Detective Welker was trying to make everyone believe. Steve also reminded me that he only takes a few cases per year, and if he thought I was lying, he would not have taken my case. When he was done talking, I had tears in my eyes. I could tell he had no doubt about me, although some of my closest friends—people I had known for years—did have some serious doubts.

CHAPTER 23

When you are involved in something life-changing, seeing how others treat you is interesting. I experienced many reactions from people, from the accusing (almost attacking) acquaintance to the supportive parents of young girls I had coached.

On one side, I had the man who confronted me at my shop where I worked building sheds. As I approached my truck to leave for the day, a car pulled into the parking lot and stopped about 40 feet from me. A middle-aged man got out and yelled, "Are you Scott?"

I replied that I was. I thought he was there to look at a shed, so I stepped forward. Then all hell almost broke loose.

He started coming at me, yelling, "You're that child molester!" I immediately refuted that claim. I shouted as fast as possible, "I never molested any child! I searched for adult pornography, and child pornography came on my computer during those searches!" Then I told him, "I have never even watched that stuff."

He stopped coming at me about 15 feet from my truck. With my quick, loud defense, something had changed slightly in his demeanor. I stopped in my tracks, turned around, and opened the door to my truck to position myself so I could get in and lock the door if he got too close. I did not need any more trouble. His next statement was interesting. "Well, you coached my daughter," he said with slightly less intensity. I said, "You're kidding. What is her name?"

He quickly said that I didn't need her name or his.

At that point, I realized he had no idea what he was doing. He was driving by and happened to see me. He had probably seen one of the many sensationalized news stories on television or in the newspaper and decided to take the law into his own hands. Perhaps common sense kicked in, and he realized that maybe, just maybe, he was wrong. But then my anger was building.

I yelled, "Well, did you ask your daughter about me? Because if you are a good parent, you should have asked her if anything was going on!" I could feel my face reddening.

He did not yell back. He quietly stated that he had talked to her, and she had said, "He was a good coach."

I told him that she was right; I was a good coach. Then I unloaded on him about DCFS, telling him that because of this, I had to pay $20 per hour to see my sons who I love more than anything.

He had one last thing to say. He looked at me and said, "Well, you always thought you were better than everyone else, so maybe this will knock you down a notch."

What? Man, did that make me angry! I think I told him he was an idiot, and he got in his car and left. Less than two minutes had passed since the altercation began. I sat in my truck, ready to explode. I wondered how many other parents of my former players and students would verbally attack me or worse.

But I thought about his words, and they hit hard. Although I was proud of my accomplishments, I had never considered myself better than anyone else. I took pride in my job, and I worked very hard. If the teams I coached were not successful, they were at least

CHAPTER 23

on their way toward that goal. I could not believe anyone would interpret that as my thinking I was better than anyone else, but this random man had exposed one of my faults. I had more pride than humility, a problem that would work itself out in the next few years.

Another reaction I encountered was people avoiding me. One day I was at Menard's, a store I had described to my sons many times as "the second happiest place on earth next to Disney." I was selecting wood for one of my building projects, and someone I'll call John was walking down the aisle toward me. He had not seen me yet, but I recognized him. We had attended the same church for many years, and about three years earlier, we were partnered up in the church golf outing. I remember him bringing a book to the outing. I think it was called *The Golfing Bible Study*. After every hole, he read a passage and a short summary tied to the game of golf. It was very cool. John seemed like a strong Christian man, and I had not seen him since my arrest.

I stopped what I was doing and turned to face him. I had always enjoyed talking with my Christian friends because they always had encouraging things to say. John got about halfway down the aisle from where I was standing. He looked at me for a moment, and our eyes made contact. I was not expecting what happened next. John had a shocked look on his face, but I only saw it for a split second because he quickly turned and walked the other way.

I know he saw me, and I was very disappointed. I wanted to yell his name out so he would have to confront me. But I had learned that staying in the background, anonymous, was usually the best idea.

I thought about John a lot that day, wondering if he was really the Christian I thought he was. After all, I might have done something wrong, but I was sure I was still a Christian. At the time, I did not realize that my actions were no better than his. He had turned his back on a brother, but I was judging him for it.

Sometimes it was not an individual but a group who acted like I had the plague. I had been attending my son's football games on Saturdays. When I first started going, I stood at one end of the sidelines as far from the other parents as possible but so I could still see the game. I wore a hat and sunglasses so I wouldn't attract attention, if that were even possible in a small community.

Many parents walked by me during the games. Some nodded and smiled, but others looked away. A group of about 10 always stood together at about the 40-yard line. None of them would acknowledge me as they walked past to get to their spot. I saw them talking, and they occasionally looked over at me. It was humiliating and frustrating. I was a parent, too, but I was not like them. They were better than me. I was a criminal.

After about five weeks, I became more comfortable going to the games. I still wore my hat but took off the sunglasses. It was too hard to see my son through the dark shades.

Some parents began to say hi as they walked by. A few of them even stopped to talk to me and see how I was doing. I was not part of their group, but I did not feel so out of place. That was until the third of five newspaper articles came out about me.

I was eating breakfast at home and reading the morning newspaper before the Saturday morning football game. There on page three was an update of my case. It covered a quarter of the page. The article detailed Detective Welker's original version of his statements against me that said I had admitted to downloading child pornography for five years. It also mentioned that forensic evidence had shown that I had watched "many of these videos numerous times."

This newspaper article came out right after Steve, Detective Welker, and I had met to clarify that those statements were false and misleading. But here were those exact incorrect words for all the public to read.

CHAPTER 23

I phoned Steve, and he got on the phone with the reporter from the newspaper. The reporter contacted the federal attorney who verified that these statements were false. Three days later, the newspaper issued a prominent retraction on page three that again covered a quarter of the page. But my issue was more immediate. I was going to my son's football game that Saturday morning.

I sported my hat and sunglasses and walked to my area on the side of the end zone—the cheap seats in a big stadium. As people walked by, it was apparent who had read their morning paper and who had not. Some people walked by me and, like always, did not give me a second look. A few people who always stopped and chatted or smiled and said hello did the same. But a few stared me down as they walked by. I was waiting for someone to say something. The group of 10 who always stood chatting at the 40-yard line had grown to over 20 people. I could see newspapers being passed around, knowing what was coming. Someone was going to ask me to leave.

I diffused the situation by going back to my truck. I waited for the game to start before I walked back toward the field. Instead of my usual spot to the side of the end zone, I stood another 40 feet back by the corner of a fence. I watched my son and returned to my truck as soon as the game ended.

I phoned my ex-wife to let her know what had happened. She was already aware. People at the game had approached her, wondering if she had seen the article. I couldn't believe a few of them actually brought the paper with them to the game. I waited in my truck for my son to give me the after-game hug I usually shared with him at the end zone.

CHAPTER 24

Not everyone treated me with aggression, avoidance, or outright rudeness. A few days after I was arrested, I found out some people truly believed in me because they had known me as more than just an acquaintance.

One night I received a phone call from a parent of two of my volleyball players. She wanted to thank me for coaching her daughters for three years. She also wanted me to know that their family had been praying for me.

I updated her on what had happened so far. She was the first to let me know that she, without any doubt, believed me. She stated that after the first newspaper article, her husband had come to her with a confession.

He also had been looking at adult pornography using the LimeWire program. He told his wife that he had seen child pornography come through and had deleted it. Due to the newspaper article about me, they had removed LimeWire and all its files from their computer. They also bought a file-cleaning program to ensure that everything was gone. This was the first of four phone calls I received where someone had the same experience as I had. I believe it would only have been a matter of time before they were caught, arrested, and prosecuted for possession.

CHAPTER 24

I never knew how someone I bumped into was going to react to me. There was no consistency among people who seemed to have similar character and morals. I experienced some churchgoing, moral people who shunned me. I also experienced the most obnoxious, beer-drinking, cursing guys who accepted me.

I experienced women who cried with me, and I experienced women who looked at me like I was a piece of garbage. I experienced acceptance from family men who had daughters and stuck up for me (thank you, Loren), just as I experienced men who would attack me if they thought they could get away with it.

I always had to be ready for anything. I could not predetermine how someone would act based on their character, morals, or church attendance. In this sad chapter of my life, I could only group people by their actions and how they treated me.

There is a saying that you will find out who your true friends are during adversity. Let me assure you that yes, you will.

Reflection Section for Chapters 18–24 available on page 217

CHAPTER 25

December 4, 2009, was my scheduled day to go to federal court for sentencing. I had plead guilty a few months earlier, and this was the day the judge would decide what my crime would cost my family and me.

Before court, I showed up at my attorney's office, and he briefed me about all the possibilities. The judge had a decision to make. Federal statutes placed the penalty range for possession of child pornography from probation to as many as 10 years in prison. Steve told me that even though probation was an option for the judge, he had never seen this judge give probation. Our judge was nicknamed Maximum Mike McCuskey. That was not encouraging information. However, Steve assured me we were in the best possible position for a favorable sentence. He outlined four things we had going for us.

First, I had told the truth the night I was arrested. More importantly, we could use the detective's own forensic report to show that I had told the truth. Steve told me that would impress the judge. Judge McCuskey, along with every other federal judge, has no tolerance for people who do not take responsibility.

Second, after looking at all the evidence, Steve said the prosecutor agreed with our explanation of how this happened.

CHAPTER 25

That would also score points with the judge. It is not beneficial to go into sentencing when you say one thing and the federal prosecutor has a different story about your case. That would force the judge to decide between an admittedly guilty criminal and a federal prosecutor who is paid to serve the public and knows justice forward and backward. It would not be a fair fight.

Third, I had asked a few people to write letters of support for me to the judge, and those people asked others to write on my behalf. Before sentencing, the judge had 45 letters of support for me. Some of the most powerful ones were from parents of children I had taught and coached. Many of them sent me copies of their letters. I was overwhelmed with the support I received.

And finally, we knew that Detective Welker would not be in court that day. His absence was one of the most important details to me. A week before, we had heard that the prosecutor had not summoned him to appear. We were certainly not going to ask him to be there.

I had thought about all the untruths Detective Welker had put in his report. We had proved them false, but each one took some time. What would happen if Detective Welker was put on the witness stand and claimed some other things we could not refute at that moment? I could only guess why the prosecutor had not asked him to be there.

If Detective Welker were called as a witness to speak for the prosecutor, my attorney would also be able to question him. Steve would have reviewed all the untruths the detective alleged in my case, discrediting him before the federal judge. The judge would have known nothing about Detective Welker or his character until that moment. I believe if that had happened, the prosecutor would not be able to use him as a witness in future cases. Since the prosecutor already had the facts and agreed with us, there was no reason to have the judge hear all the previous theories.

Again, that is only my guess. In any case, it was favorable that the arresting detective and investigator would be absent from the courtroom.

After Steve explained why we were in the best place we could be, we reviewed the federal guidelines. In federal court, the judge is given sentencing guidelines set by Congress. Although many factors figured in, those guidelines indicated the typical prison sentence range I would receive for my specific crime. The standard punishment for my offense was between 97 and 120 months in prison. That would be eight to 10 years away from my sons.

I was shocked by this information. I knew the guidelines would fall between probation and 10 years. But I could not believe that after figuring in the details of my case I would be in the upper level of that range. Steve informed me that intent is not part of the formula.

There was a bit of good news that went along with this. Another part of the guidelines includes what is called the "mandatory minimum." The typical mandatory minimum for my crime is five years. That means that no matter how much the judge likes me, he had to give me at least five years in prison. Months earlier, we learned I was not being hit with the five-year mandatory minimum. That was some good news!

After Steve and I met, we headed to the federal courthouse to find out my fate. I was surprised to walk into the lobby and find many friends waiting for me. I was even more surprised when I entered the courtroom and found people already inside. Between 40 and 50 of my supporters were in the courtroom.

There were friends I had known for 20 years. I had met them in Jaycees when life was about raising money through projects such as the annual haunted house and then using that money to take needy children shopping for presents at Christmas.

CHAPTER 25

There were parents of my former volleyball players there. Some of them had only known me for two or three years, but they appreciated me as a coach for their daughters and believed in my character.

There were some people there from my church. The youth pastor who lived across the street from our family was there for me, as he had been the entire time. He was always available to talk to me when I saw him or called him. More importantly, he played with my sons in the yard after school many days when I could not.

Not everyone in the courtroom was my supporter. Right behind me sat two detectives from Decatur, one from my neighborhood. I was glad that neither of them was Detective Welker.

After I sat down, I recognized someone sitting in the front row with a pad of paper, a pencil, and a tape recorder. This reporter had been grossly misled months earlier and had written that awful newspaper article for everyone to read on a Saturday morning before my son's football game. He was the reporter who put in the prominent retraction three days later and then accurately reported the facts. He was there in the courtroom to get the truth firsthand. I appreciated that.

I must add that his article in the newspaper the next day was very accurate. He did a great job of covering what happened. It was the last article he would write. That night he died in his home of carbon monoxide poisoning from a problem with his furnace. The newspaper suffered a significant loss with his passing.

CHAPTER 26

Sentencing lasted a couple of hours. The judge started by welcoming all my supporters and stating why we were there. Then there was some legal stuff the attorneys had to work out regarding how many points I was being charged with. Points are what determine the guideline range. My attorney was challenging three areas that added points to my sentencing spectrum. We lost all three challenges. The guideline range remained 97 to 120 months. Then it was time for the Decatur detectives.

Judge McCuskey had a standing policy in these cases that the court would show a small portion of an illegal video found on the defendant's computer. He said he does this because some defendants lie and tell their supporters, "I thought she was eighteen," or "I did not know she was underage." Judge McCuskey wanted my supporters to understand the seriousness of what was found.

The detectives were there with a copy of a video found on my computer. It was hooked to the court's video player and on the big screen for all to see.

I did not watch. I had no doubt the detectives would bring the worst possible example of an illegal video. I did not doubt that it was somewhere on my computer. I looked away from the screen for the 30 seconds the judge allowed this to happen.

CHAPTER 26

After addressing some legal matters, Steve called the first of our two witnesses. He started by calling the psychologist I had been seeing for over a year. Dr. Wentz went on the stand for two reasons.

First, he shared about his time spent with me and what his findings were. His opinions were positive for my case. The second reason he was there was to share the findings of the government's psychologist who evaluated me about 10 months earlier. The government-assigned psychologist, Dr. Kleppin, had put me through a battery of tests that took just under eight hours. It was fascinating. The federal probation officer set up the evaluation. It was her job to ensure the public was safe if I was going out on bond with very few restrictions.

Dr. Kleppin's report was short at 18 pages, but it needed a translator such as Dr. Wentz due to the many technical words the highly educated government psychologist used. Dr. Wentz shared with the court that Dr. Kleppin had found that I exhibited no sexual desire toward children. He also told the judge I was in the "least likely category ever to commit a crime again."

I thought that was a powerful statement. Dr. Wentz found that I was as likely to commit another crime as was, well, the judge or the prosecutor. He stated they never deemed anyone with no chance of ever committing a crime. Being in the least likely range was as good as it gets. I'll gladly take that label.

The second witness Steve called to the stand was my brother Mark. He owns a computer company, and the prosecutor accepted him as an expert witness. Mark told the court how the LimeWire program works. He also stated that he was the one who originally put the program on my computer at my request. He stated that when LimeWire first came out, he did not consider it dangerous. But now, all kinds of videos were available, including illegal ones. He also confirmed that the dangerous part of LimeWire was that video names and descriptions could be changed. There was no way to be 100 percent sure of what you were getting until you got it.

After our two witnesses, it was the prosecutor's turn to call witnesses. He did not. He had previously told Steve he would not challenge our account of what happened. He did not try to make this out to be anything other than what it was.

Once the witnesses finished, it was time for the prosecutor and my attorney to make final statements. The prosecutor went first. He began with why we were there. He never got out his second sentence before the judge interrupted him.

Judge McCuskey said we were there because the police in Decatur wanted my case to be given more prison time than I would have gotten if it had stayed in the state court system. He went on to say that if I were in the state system, I would have probably gotten probation. I was brought here for a higher sentence. The judge stated my case did not deserve to be in federal court, but now that it was, he would do what he felt was right. This blew me away. It was a short attack on Detective Welker and everyone else involved in making my case go federal. I thought of the other six men who got arrested for the same crime within two weeks of my arrest. They all stayed in state court and received various lengths of probation. But here I was in federal court with the possibility of 10 years in prison. And the judge just pointed that out to everyone in the courtroom.

Judge McCuskey finished his interruption of the prosecutor by assuring him that the chance of a higher sentence was the only reason I was brought to federal court and warned him not to state it was for any other reason.

This felt like a monumental turn of events for me. I had felt for months that there was no reason for me to be in federal court. I felt like the only reason I was there was because I lived in a

CHAPTER 26

neighborhood with so many police officers. They wanted to make a point that this would not happen around them without severe consequences.

I also felt that this had happened because I was a teacher, and the officers knew the added publicity would bring potential victims out into the open. But I knew there were no victims to come out.

I did not recognize any solid reason to bring my case to federal court. And now the judge had just confirmed that my case should have been handled in state court. This was the first time that day that I thought I was getting probation from Judge McCuskey, as did many of my supporters.

When the prosecutor continued, he covered a few general facts about these crimes. He also talked a little about the testimonies of Dr. Wentz and my brother Mark. He attempted to finish his summary with a bang. He finished his statement by talking about the number of illegal videos in my possession. He stated a number that was the biggest I had heard yet. Then he put a twist on it.

He said I possessed 254 movies and 15 other images of the illegal videos. Then he stated that this was over 10 hours of child pornography. The prosecutor did not elaborate on that claim. He threw it out for effect, but Steve would quickly clarify this for the court.

CHAPTER 27

After the prosecutor sat down, Judge McCuskey called Steve to take his turn and address what the prosecutor had said. Steve started with the claim of 254 videos. He reminded the judge of a few facts regarding the prosecutor's statement. That number—254—was actually a double number. Detective Welker's final tally claimed that there were 129 movies on the computer. But I had a backup drive from my previous computer that they also took from my home. Detective Welker claimed this backup drive had 125 movies on it. So the prosecutor had counted both drives together. In fact, we were able to show that 95 percent of the movies on my current computer were copies from my previous computer.

When my brother set up my new computer, he told me to keep a copy of my old hard drive-in case my new computer crashed. I did that. My brother had confirmed this in his testimony just an hour before.

I had put this hard drive in my computer table drawer and left it there. I had not touched it in over two years. All the videos on my current computer hard drive were from two years before with the addition of four more. As I told the detective the night I was arrested, I did not use LimeWire much anymore. The forensic

CHAPTER 27

report confirmed that the videos from over two years ago had not been reopened after the initial download when I saw what they were and thought I had deleted them. Steve covered all this thoroughly for the court.

Steve continued addressing several other points. First, he said I had not attempted to minimize my conduct. He stated that I had spent the time since my arrest talking to anyone who would listen about the dangers of Internet pornography to prevent them from getting caught up in the same circumstances.

He explained how men used to walk into dirty bookstores and pick out precisely what they were looking for. Now, with the Internet, we have no idea what we are getting until we get it. And then it is too late.

He pointed out that the law says if you have fewer than three illegal images on your computer you can self-report to law enforcement and not suffer any penalty. However, just one video counts as 75 images. So there is no defense for someone like myself who did broad searches and attempted to delete what I did not want.

Next, Steve explained that the judge could give me a sentence less than the low end of the guideline (97 months) without setting a precedent. He mentioned that judges across the country were beginning to give lower than guideline sentences in cases like this because they determined that the guidelines were too high. He then said that the court should look at me. These were his words directly from the court transcript:

> Well, what about this defendant? We've got a defendant who was a schoolteacher. It took him a while to get there. He went to college on the installment plan, but ultimately, he became a schoolteacher. He was a good schoolteacher, and he became a coach. He was a

EXEMPLARY LIFE

good coach. He cared; he coached girls' volleyball—interestingly, young girls. He was a good coach. He cared for his players. He cared for his team. They achieved success. They were proud of themselves. Many of them went on to college.

You [the prosecutor] said you entered a forfeiture order. I didn't even get a chance to object because you just broadly forfeited everything that was there. There were four videotapes that they took. They were recruiting tapes. They were tapes that he had put together so that his girls could—that had played in high school—could get scholarships to go to college. That's the kind of coach he was. And many of the letters that you have are from parents or other people in the school system that recognized the kind of commitment that Scott made as a, as a teacher and as a coach.

Steve then took a minute to talk about my computer. He stated that investigators are just looking for computers that have illegal videos, and they do not look at the situation. He explained that my one computer had over 500 legal videos from years of downloading. There were pornography movies along with music videos, television episodes, comedy shows—all kinds of videos. He noted that this indiscriminate use of the Internet is the problem.

Steve then shared these words on my conduct after my arrest:

> Well, so what happens? Because you have to pay the piper. If you're going to engage in criminal behavior as Scott does, you have to pay the piper. He gets arrested and charged in Decatur. Boom! His wife leaves him. He gets a divorce. Boom! He loses his job.

CHAPTER 27

And now unfortunately, you know, he had to move in with his mother, and now his mother has died.

But I think that when you have a crisis in your life, how you respond to that crisis tells you a lot about the character of the individual before the Court. Scott did not whine. Scott has not said to anyone, "Oh, it was, you know, an accident." He acknowledges his indiscriminate use and search for pornography is what got him in trouble, and he's accepted responsibility for what he did. But that's what he did. Let's not sentence him because of something somebody else did or because somebody else who collects child pornography won't come in here and tell you that they collect child pornography. Let's sentence him for what he did.

Well, what, what has he done after these charges?

He's committed himself to his business. He's met his financial obligations—he's tried to—and is getting on with his life. A sentence of imprisonment ends that, Judge. Now, a sentence of imprisonment sends the message to all the world, "Don't you dare indiscriminately use the computer to access pornography because you're committing a crime, and when you commit that crime, you are harming kids" because that's what indiscriminate use of the Internet does. It ultimately harms kids.

Steve's next point was to talk about the sentencing. He pointed out that of the 1,519 men who got sentenced last year for possession of child pornography, only 1 percent got probation.

Two things caught my attention. In one year, 1,519 people got sentenced for the same crime. And that is just in federal court.

That number does not include state courts. That calculates to over four men every day just for this one crime. The second thing that came to my mind was that my chance of getting probation from Maximum Mike McCuskey was slim to none.

Steve finished by again pointing out that the guidelines, although accurately calculated here, hit my case way too hard. He told the judge that he should not follow the guidelines in my case. But if the judge felt imprisonment was necessary, he could fashion a split sentence of six months in prison and then six months of home confinement. This sentence would be an effective punishment that would keep me close to my sons. Steve thanked the court and sat down.

Immediately the prosecutor said, "Judge, I would like to respond." That worried me. I thought he had his chance already.

The judge said, "Okay. And then I'll give Mr. Beckett a chance to respond after that."

CHAPTER 28

The prosecutor walked up to the podium and announced that he had four quick points regarding what my attorney had said. His first point was that my attorney is "really very, very, good." I thought to myself, well, that is nice. Thank you.

The second point he wanted to address was the statistics. He had a minor issue with my attorney claiming that almost half of the sentences last year for this crime resulted in a less than guideline sentence. He wanted the court to know that those are not statistics for our judge but for the entire country. Then he reminded Judge McCuskey of his record.

The prosecutor stated, "And if you don't know your own stats, you're usually within 10, or maybe 15 percent is the most you go. You're usually within about 10 percent of the guideline range."

This was not a positive statement for me. Steve had told me that my chances of getting probation were not good. But I had no idea that Judge McCuskey never differed more than 15% from the guidelines. I quickly scribbled the numbers on my scratch paper at the table. Fifteen percent off of a 97-month sentence is 82 months. That's almost seven years in prison if the judge gives me his best deal.

The third point the prosecutor made was unbelievable to me. He said, "We're not here . . . to contest whether or not Mr. Brown is a pedophile. I never used that word. The only person that used that word was Mr. Beckett. He is not a pedophile." This was in reference to Steve's statement early in his presentation that "the government would lead the court to believe that I was a pedophile."

I had come to understand very early on that the job of the prosecutor was to present me as guilty. His role was to be the enemy. We were on different teams. My experience with the detective part of the other team was that the other team would stretch the truth if they could make things go against me. But here, in the game's final moments, the prosecuting attorney had just defended me. He could have left this comment by my attorney alone. He could have let the word *pedophile* slide by subliminally, hoping it would hook into the judge's mind. But he clarified his view of me. "He is not a pedophile." With that one sentence, he gained my respect.

The prosecutor did not get to his fourth point. He started, but he did not get to finish it. He began by saying something about why we were here today. The judge immediately interrupted him to tell him again that we were here today because someone in Decatur wanted a higher sentence for me. The prosecutor tried to go back to that thought a few times when the judge was done speaking, but each time the judge interrupted him with more vigor. This entire exchange took up five full pages of the transcript.

To summarize, Judge McCuskey challenges the prosecutor that we are here, in fact, for a higher sentence. When the prosecutor, Mr. Bruce, disagrees, the judge asks, "So they have a higher statutory penalty? That would be more than 120 months in Decatur?"

Mr. Bruce starts to answer by stuttering, "Your honor, I—no. I'll tell you the answer to that question." But then the judge cuts him off again. Judge McCuskey goes on to say that he has a higher

CHAPTER 28

case load right now than he has ever had. And he points out that the problem is that the ones bringing the cases to his courtroom are not federal agents. They are employees of the cities and the counties. Clearly, he is not happy about it and stares directly at the two Decatur police officers sitting in the front row.

Now for a third time, Mr. Bruce starts with, "Judge, I'll—I guess, you know, you should never disagree with the judge when asking for a sentence, but I am going to disagree with you. We're here because—" and the judge cuts him off.

Judge McCuskey refers to all the cases being brought to his courtroom and that if the state guys are going to keep bringing them here for higher sentences, he should be making more money. He continues that he made more money as a state judge and did not understand why.

Mr. Bruce starts to speak, and the judge interrupts him again, saying, "Higher workload, less pay." There is a chuckle from the people in the courtroom.

Mr. Bruce decides to go with this and replies, "Since your salary and the U.S. Attorney's salary directly impact my salary, I would love it if you got paid a lot more because then I would get paid a lot more money."

The judge then begins to talk about his workload again. He says if he calls his state buddies at 3:00 this afternoon, they would all be gone but that he would be in his office until 5:00 every night. Then the judge looks at the reporter and says, "I hope they put that in the paper." This elicits another bit of laughter from the crowded gallery.

Judge McCuskey continues by saying he is there until after 5:00 every night and "would like to go to Macon County and see if I could get into the building after 5:00."

By that time, Mr. Bruce had lost his train of thought and was attempting to get back on track. He began to talk about these types of cases and the variation you see in sentencing at the state court level. The judge interrupts and says, "They also don't spend two hours sentencing anybody, do they?"

Mr. Bruce decides to complete his sentencing thought again and gives a reason for the two-hour sentencing. During this thought, he mentions Kankakee, Illinois. The judge gets his biggest laugh of the afternoon.

Judge McCuskey interrupts Mr. Bruce and says, "They did invite me to their Christmas party, though."

Mr. Bruce responds, "Kankakee did?"

And the judge replies, "Yes, they did. I've never been invited to Decatur's Christmas party." At that point, even I have a smile on my face.

Mr. Bruce's half thoughts continue for about two more minutes, with the judge interrupting about not being paid, what state judges gets paid, and how there has been additional money for new prosecutors but not judges. Finally, Mr. Bruce finishes by stating that we are here today because Congress has told him to focus on these cases. Fifteen years ago, the focus was on firearms. Ten years ago, it was crack. And now, it is child pornography. These are the cases that should now be hit the hardest. With that, Mr. Bruce sat down for the last time, and the judge awarded my attorney a chance to respond.

Steve starts by again defending the statistics he presented. Almost half of the 1,519 pornography cases received a sentence below the guidelines. Then Steve makes sure Judge McCuskey knows Detective Welker has not been truthful about what happened in my case. But he does it more subtly than I would have. He says this:

> You know, when we did the plea, Judge, there had— in the plea agreement, there had been a, a factual error. And Agent—Agent Welker and Mr. Bruce and

CHAPTER 28

I got together, and we corrected it to make sure that you were aware. Because all Agent Welker could tell us is that there were some files that had been opened, and all he could show was that they'd been opened one time. And I'm telling you, that's exactly what happened in this case. The indiscriminate use of pornography means that these stupid males, these stupid males who use the Internet, bring tons of child pornography to their computers; and they think in their stupid brains that when they start viewing it and they see that crud and they delete it that they're not possessing child pornography. That's not true. They are.

At this point, my attorney sat down. I was thinking to myself, I wish I could be that clear with my thoughts. The only thing I would have changed was when he called Detective Welker's affidavit a factual error. I would have called it a lie. But Judge McCuskey understood what Steve meant.

The judge then came to the last speaker of the day before deciding what kind of sentence he would hand down. He announced that I could take the podium if I wished to address the court. That is called the allocution, and it was my last chance to make an impression on the judge. I had learned that Judge McCuskey does not make his final decision on sentencing until he hears what the defendant has to say. So this was my last chance to influence his decision.

CHAPTER 29

An allocution can sway a judge. I believe it can persuade negatively more than positively. When it was time for me to give my allocution, Judge McCuskey already knew everything about me and my actions. He wanted to hear my thoughts, in my own words.

I believed that if I got up and accepted responsibility for what happened as I had from the beginning, the judge would appreciate that. He would go close to the sentence he had already been considering.

I was not going to change my story. I was not going to call it an accident or say I ignored the illegal videos when they came to my computer. Even though I knew my searches might bring them in, I had continued my actions. That was not an accident. That was carelessness. I accepted that and was genuinely sorry. I wanted Judge McCuskey to know that.

I also believe that if I had changed my tune and denied guilt in this case, Judge McCuskey would have given me the whole 10 years in prison. I wrote my allocution speech to take responsibility and ask the judge for mercy.

The following is my allocution taken from the transcript of my sentencing day.

CHAPTER 29

I'm here today because I knowingly had child pornography on my computer. I had child pornography come to my computer while searching for adult pornography. I was looking for specific types of young women. The search terms I used produced all kinds of pornography, including child pornography. Even though I knew I had child pornography on my computer, I did nothing about it except delete the files I could preview.

Child pornography represents abused children. This abuse is magnified when the video is sent out over the Internet. I now realize that my downloading of child pornography was contributing to the abuse of these children. If there's no market for the material, the material will stop being made. The thought of someone abusing a child because I contributed to the market distresses me.

I dedicated 13 years of my life to helping young people as a teacher, a coach, an athletic director, and a father. I have worked very hard to help my students, athletes, and sons succeed. My teaching and coaching record is flawless. I never imagined that my carelessness was contributing to people abusing the very children that I was trying to help.

My conduct has caused me to lose my wife of 14 years, who I love very much. My conduct caused me to lose my career and the passion I loved, teaching and coaching. I feel like it's what I was born to do. I spent so many years building a great reputation, and I hate that I destroyed it with this conduct. I spent years teaching my players good moral judgment so they could be a part of the team I was coaching, and I've set an awful example.

Most importantly, my conduct has damaged my two young sons. I love my sons more than anything in this world. I grew up without a father. I never wanted my boys to grow up without a father in their lives. I remember teaching my sons how to throw a knuckleball in the backyard at our house. That night at prayers, my older son said, "Your dad never taught you to throw a knuckleball, did he?"

He knows my dad left when I was five. I remember telling him that my dad never taught me how to throw a knuckleball and that they would never have to worry about my leaving because Mommy and I would always be here for him. I feel like I've broken my promise to my sons.

As a Monday morning quarterback, I ask myself how this could have happened. Child pornography is in the news every day. I should have seen the dangers of Internet pornography. Since my arrest, I've repeatedly talked to other men about the damages and dangers of Internet pornography.

Judge McCuskey, I want to do my part to correct this growing problem. I cannot undo the damage I have done to my wife and sons. I cannot undo the damage that I did to my career and reputation. And I cannot undo the damage I did to my returning players who expected to return to state competition. Teachers and coaches have a special responsibility to their students and players. While I cannot undo the damage I've done to mine, I can help other men from damaging any other children by helping them realize this danger.

CHAPTER 29

> I am asking your trust as a coach and a teacher that I can motivate other men in keeping them—and keep them from coming before you as I have had to today. Thank you.

Judge McCuskey followed my allocution with the following comments.

> Thank you, Mr. Brown. . . . So I appreciate what you just did, Scott. You admitted and accepted responsibility. We have people who do not accept responsibility, ministers who lie to congregations, people who cause divorces by lying to families, people who, in front of a judge, blame the government, people who take the stand and say, "Well, somebody put it there. I didn't."
>
> We rarely have an acceptance of responsibility, a true acceptance, and I appreciate the fact you—what you said today and what you said immediately when confronted.

During this time, the judge was looking directly at me. He was talking to me. None of the lawyers or supporters existed. He was letting me know that he had listened to what I said and was taking it into account. This was another reason I respected Judge McCuskey.

I want to take a moment to address something I said in my allocution. Right near the beginning, I said, "I now realize how my downloading of child pornography was contributing to the abuse of these children. If there's no market for the material, the material will stop being made. The thought of someone abusing a child because I contributed to the market distresses me."

A few moments later, I reiterated, "I never imagined that my carelessness was contributing to people abusing the very children I was trying to help."

Some of you may read this story and ask yourself how I was contributing to the market. As I was downloading adult pornography, these illegal videos were also coming through. I did not share any videos with anyone. I never purchased any videos or joined a website. But just because nothing was purchased or exchanged does not cancel the fact that my actions contributed to the abuse of these children.

I am just one of literally thousands of men who have been arrested for possession of child pornography. In 2007 alone, over 1,500 people, mostly men, were arrested for this crime. It is a wildfire out of control. Even though there was nothing of value being exchanged in my case, the sheer numbers show that there is a market. And I became part of that market.

I also believe that my actions contributed to the abuse of these children. Right after my arrest, the story was all over the television news, and five newspaper articles were written about me. My actions caused this to happen. My activities became newsworthy.

There are millions of children in our world who are being abused every day. Some of those children may live in my hometown. Some of those children may have known and respected me. It had to be doubly painful for them when they saw or heard the news of my arrest.

I was a respected man. I was someone they trusted. And now I was just another adult male they could not believe in anymore. I cannot imagine the pain I must have caused them.

My actions have affected many others. My sons and I had a great relationship. I loved playing with them and teaching them things every day. I was an active parent. As I write today, I am

CHAPTER 29

missing out on a large part of my sons' lives. They are growing up without a dad, just as I did.

My actions damaged my ex-wife. With dating and marriage, she had spent over 20 years with me. We started as a young couple with day-to-day jobs and lived in a tiny, one-bedroom apartment. We worked up to being two responsible adults with careers that helped the youth of Decatur. The entire time, my ex-wife loved me. Now because of my actions, she has hate in her heart for me. I have prayed so often for that hate to go away.

My actions did contribute negatively to young people. Some of the students at the schools where I taught had bonded with me. I was the only coach and father figure some of those kids had. They were in my physical education classes from kindergarten through sixth grade. At one of my other schools, I had boys and girls I had coached in track or volleyball from fourth through eighth grades. These kids relied on me to be a positive part of their lives.

Too often, kids across the nation are let down by the male adults in their lives. I was one of the few adult males in the schools where I taught. For some of these kids, I was the only adult male for whom they had respect. I am so sorry this happened. I let them all down.

CHAPTER 30

After my allocution and, more importantly, Judge McCuskey's acceptance of my allocution, it came time for my sentence.

The judge covered points of the case from the beginning to the end. He began by discussing my arrest on July 18, 2008, and my interview with Detective Welker. I discovered the detective had one more surprise for me.

The judge said I admitted to downloading pornography using LimeWire and Kazaa's file-sharing programs. Then he said that I did this by using search terms such as *Lolita*, *pedo*, and *small tits* when searching for pornography files. I was waiting for the other terms, but the judge did not mention any others. Later, I found out by looking at Detective Welker's affidavit that he did not include any others. He used a few terms that would help his case and left the others out.

I told Detective Welker about 10 or 15 search terms I had used. At the time just before my arrest, the only search term I was using was *new porn* because I was tired of getting the same videos I had received hundreds of times over five years. I told Detective Welker that I had also searched for *blonde*, *long legs*, *cute girl*, and many other general search terms. If I saw a video

CHAPTER 30

I wanted to see more of, I searched whatever words were in the description. There were some terms such as *qwerty* and *asdf* that I still don't know how they connect to any pornography. But they were there as descriptions, so I occasionally searched them. But the only ones that Detective Welker put in his report were *Lolita*, *pedo*, and *small tits*. That was not surprising.

Judge McCuskey continued by covering the history of this type of crime. He described the first case he had tried, which involved mail order. There was no Internet back then. He said they caught the defendant with the videotape in the player just 15 minutes after the delivery was made. He continued to say that the defendant then made his biggest blunder. He brought his entire family to court, including his young children. Then the defendant talked about it being a victimless crime. He wanted his grandchildren and daughters to hear that. Judge McCuskey did not give that man a favorable sentence.

Judge McCuskey talked about how the children in these videos are ruined for life. And that is the reason there is a statute against these crimes. He then said that "the only issue is the appropriate punishment." Here we go.

I was still hopeful at this point that I was going to get probation. Judge McCuskey quickly made it clear that was not going to happen. These were his words:

> But I want it clear. It's going to be difficult for me ever to find the facts or the case that imprisonment is not the punishment. I cannot see—maybe it will happen someday—I have never given probation in one of these cases. There has to be a punishment. I don't think there could be a State Court Judge who has come before me who could believe that this was probationable.

EXEMPLARY LIFE

I was thinking to myself, you are wrong, Judge. My case is probationable. Like my attorney said, "This defendant is different." I may have been careless, but I am not a threat to society—not any part of it. Even the prosecutor agreed with that.

The judge continued:

> So what is the appropriate punishment within a range that goes up to 120 months? I have to look at the statutory factors. I have to look at not only what I've been talking about, of course, which is the nature and circumstances of this horrible offense—a crime against children that lasts forever, thanks to the Internet and video—but also the character and history of the defendant for an appropriate sentence under 18 United States Code 3553 (a), sufficient, not greater than necessary, appropriate and reasonable.

This was the second time that day I heard those words—sufficient, not greater than necessary, appropriate and reasonable. I felt that probation would be all those things after all that I had already lost from of my life.

Next, the judge talked about how my case hits close to home. Judge McCuskey is a former teacher and coach. His sister just retired from teaching. His grandmother taught until she was 70 years old. And his dad was a coach.

Judge McCuskey said this:

> And what I heard today from Scott is basically what my dad told me. Teachers and coaches have a special responsibility to students, the people they coach, and—my dad said—society. He said teachers are right up there with ministers, priests, and rabbis: the

CHAPTER 30

people who mold society to be better, the people who make our society better.

And then my dad said—and I've never forgotten it—lawyers don't do any of those things. Lawyers are the people who steal without even having a mask.

In another setting, Judge McCuskey would have received a standing ovation at this point. But here, he got another polite laugh from the gallery.

Now Judge McCuskey turned his attention to me. He looked right at me, and the courtroom disappeared for me. He was going to talk to me. I had heard about this talk from others who had experienced the wrath of a federal judge. This is where he rips you apart and lets you know how badly you have screwed up. I was emotionally not ready.

Judge McCuskey went on:

> So when I read the letters, Scott, as I do in each and every case, I was glad to read the letters, especially from the women who trusted you with their daughters and from those daughters who grew up to think that you specially served them and that no one knew about this "Late Night Scott." They didn't know about it. And that's good because they never saw anything that would let them down.
>
> So I have to look at your character and history. And while I've made it clear that character and history could never lead me in a child pornography case—not as exemplary as your coaching and teaching had been—to probation, it certainly weighs heavily on what is an appropriate and reasonable sentence, sufficient, but not greater than necessary.

Well, I thought, that wasn't too bad. But Judge McCuskey was not finished. He continued. He talked about how most of the time he follows the sentencing guidelines. He described how in drug cases, some kids are selling $10 crack, and the agent will say, "Let's just plead to five grams." And the kid does not understand what that means. They don't realize it becomes a federal case punishable by a minimum of five to 10 years in federal prison. And the judge said, "You couldn't possibly get that in Decatur."

He continued with his earlier thought:

> So I know that some people clearly come to federal court for high sentences since most of my cases are drugs and guns, and they're brought here by police and deputy sheriffs and not federal agents. And child pornography probably is here for the same reason. But I accept that responsibility gladly because somebody has to send a message.

The next part of Judge McCuskey's speech was when I realized I was not getting probation. He said, "And the message is: If Scott Brown, with his exemplary life, goes to prison for child pornography, maybe that means everyone will."

I was very mixed up at this point. The judge was complimenting me on my "exemplary life" but would use me to send a message. I was thinking to myself that the message had already been sent. Everyone I knew had seen that I had lost my family and career. To whom was this message to be sent? The judge then cleared it up like this:

> Maybe that means there should be a warning in every handbook given out with a computer. This is a dangerous instrument because child pornography

CHAPTER 30

will be punished seriously; and if you're caught with it, and you don't go to the police and tell them, you'll go to prison." [Of course, if you are caught with even one video that slipped through, that is 75 images, and you can still go to prison by telling the police about it.] So I hope, if anything, the message in Decatur is being spread that this is what happens, no matter how exemplary your life.

So the message was to the people of Decatur. But with that statement, he did it again. He mentioned my exemplary life. I was expecting him to chew me out, but he kept stating what a great life I have had. I was still unsure how much of the 10 years in prison I was getting.

Next, Judge McCuskey covered his responsibilities. He told the court that the guidelines used to be mandatory, but now they are not. He has the ability to go outside of the 97-month to 120-month range. He stated that the Supreme Court gave him that discretion, allowing him to "truly look at the character and history of a defendant and truly look at appropriate and reasonable punishment."

This was at least the third time he said that the sentence he was about to give me would be "appropriate and reasonable." A few times he included "not greater than necessary." I have always wondered why Judge McCuskey would refer to this so often.

I believe it was to show on the record that he was taking this sentence seriously, that he put a lot of thought into my sentence. I do feel Judge McCuskey believed he would give me precisely the punishment needed to pay for my crime.

The second responsibility Judge McCuskey stated was his duty to protect the public. He said it this way: "Protect the public from further crimes of the defendant. I've read the letters. I heard the allocution. There's no way that Scott's going to be a criminal. He never was. He won't be again."

There is no way to interpret what Judge McCuskey said incorrectly. He had no reason to believe that I would be a criminal. I never was a criminal. I never will be a criminal. He got that right. But still, I must pay for the crime I did commit.

After stating I was not a criminal, he said, "So part of your sentence, Scott, is to send a message. And I hope the message is clear. If you use child pornography and you're caught, you will go to prison." Again, the judge was using me to send a message to those who actually use child pornography.

The judge's third responsibility is to think about the defendant. "Offer the opportunity for rehabilitation. Scott's already on the road to rehabilitation. We know that from counseling. We know that from the psychological reports."

My attorney, Steve, had addressed this perfectly earlier in the proceedings. He stated that he had "committed himself to his business. He's met his financial obligations—he's tried to—and is getting on with his life. A sentence of imprisonment ends that." I had hoped the judge would weigh that along with all the time I had devoted to raising my sons.

The fourth responsibility that Judge McCuskey shared with the courtroom was to give a sentence that was consistent and fair. Right before pronouncing my sentence, he used this moment to show the court how hard he could be. He continued:

> And a sentence should ensure consistent, fair, determinate, and proportional sentences. Those people who won't accept responsibility, who go to trial and lie to a jury, who come before me for sentencing and lie again, and lie to their family and friends—and I get letters where I know that they've lied. Those

CHAPTER 30

people in every case have received a maximum sentence, and I don't go to bed at night and feel sorry for them or lose one minute of sleep. They deserve the maximum sentence when they think they can lie to everybody in the system from beginning to end and bring people into my courtroom who think somehow the government or the police or somebody else put it on their computer. They're just an accidental victim of the system being ground up. Those people deserve swift, harsh punishment.

And with that, Judge McCuskey was done listing his responsibilities in fashioning my sentence. How glad I am that I had told the truth from day one. I do not doubt that if I had played any foolish games with my story, Judge Maximum Mike McCuskey would have shown me the door with a 10-year sentence.

CHAPTER 31

Judge McCuskey now moved to sentencing. There are a few things I did not understand, but now, after reviewing it many times, it has become more apparent. I will do my best to explain the relativeness of the judge's comments.

He began sentencing by saying, "Now, Mr. Bruce [the prosecutor], you ended up with 90 months. But Mr. Kistner [from probation] recommended to me 78 months. He said that he felt there should be a reduction in the sentence because Mr. Scott Brown was not actively file-sharing or trading, and he recommended 78."

I need to interject something about Mr. Kistner. My attorney warned me that he usually finds more points in the advisory guidelines than the government can find. People think they're going to get a shorter sentence, and Mr. Kistner comes in and says, "You missed it. It should be about 10 years more than you thought."

The judge continued:

> I believe both the government and Mr. Kistner are too high. I cannot overlook the character and history of this defendant. I cannot overlook his remorse, which is clear in the letters, his openness, and the fact

CHAPTER 31

> that he admitted to people what most people don't do. That shows me that he has a very strong character now, in spite—and is willing to admit—in spite of the offense and willingness to admit his failure, his shameful conduct, which he openly admits. So if anybody wants a formula, Mr. Beckett, for the future, it's not a formula for me to be concerned about other judges in any circuit.

This was in reference to Steve's statistics about what judges were doing across the country.

I would later fully understand the weight of Mr. Bruce's and Mr. Kistner's recommendations. Others I shared this with thought that a prosecutor would never go below the guidelines. His job was to get the highest sentence he thought he could get. In my case, Mr. Bruce recommended approximately 10 percent off the guideline range of 97 months.

I would also learn that many people don't tell the exact truth when they are first confronted. The judge commented that they "rarely have an acceptance of responsibility, a true acceptance."

This was Judge McCuskey's courtroom. No one else's. So he went on:

> It's [the formula] for people to be concerned with the true character of who's before me. I'm sentencing an individual here based on who he is, not what some judge did to somebody last month in California or New York or even what some judge did in Springfield or Peoria. Sentencing is still individually based, as the Supreme Court has allowed me to look at these circumstances and determine an appropriate and reasonable sentence and sufficient, not greater than necessary.

This was just the first part of the judge's lesson on "the formula" for a lighter sentence. The second part would arrive soon enough. But first, Judge McCuskey decided to address my attorney's suggestion.

> It would depreciate the seriousness of this offense and the victims for me to say, "Yes, we'll do a 12-month split sentence." I wouldn't sleep at night. I would feel that I have missed my calling. My calling is to do justice for the people, to deter, to promote respect for the law, as well as for Scott Brown.

I believe my attorney was originally going to suggest probation, but as the proceedings went on, he realized the judge would not accept that and asked for a 12-month split sentence. It was Steve's way of trying to mitigate the damages. I felt my actions deserved probation, but soon enough, we would all know what the judge felt.

> So, in looking at this case, I believe that basically, the guidelines were 97 to 120 months. Mr. Bruce, I won't tell the government that you've varied from the guidelines. You can blame it on me. I won't tell the government that Mr. Kistner varied from the guidelines. You can blame it on me. I believe that basically, in this case, this is a sentence that should be approximately half of the guidelines.

CHAPTER 32

Judge McCuskey had just announced that I was getting a sentence valued at about half of what the guidelines suggest. At that moment, I realized I was going to go to prison. I did not turn around to look at my supporters. And at first, I could not hear them. But after a few moments, I began to hear the sniffling noise that goes with crying. Not everyone, but a few were doing what I could not.

I did not cry. I had no tears in my eyes. I was utterly stunned. I never guessed that my carelessness would take me away from my sons. I had not considered whether this was half of the 97 months or the 120 months.

Judge McCuskey went on to give his reason for his decision. "This is not a person actively file-sharing. It is not a person dealing it, and if you want, we will show it." He was referring to the video the police brought with them to the courtroom. The judge continued.

> Because most child pornography cases deal with adults having sex with three- and four-year-old children, bound and gagged, treated like a piece of meat along the road that they found like they're roadkill. Horrible. And if the government was

going to show it to me, today was the time. But it didn't happen. So I do not believe this is the worst form of child pornography that we show to jurors that make them sick and want to throw up.

I have to also look at the nature and circumstances of this offense, these facts. So the formula for receiving a lower-than-guideline sentence is: Own up to it quick. Be honest about who you are and what you've done to your family and friends, and don't come in here and jam the system, jack it around with a trial that you lie at and then come in here and don't accept responsibility. That is a formula for a maximum sentence. That would be a formula for me saying, "Mr. Bruce, you've got it wrong. It's 120 months. It's the whole ball of wax." I've done it before. And I'll do it again in those cases.

But, Mr. Brown, you have impressed the court. I'm sure you'll walk out of here and say, "Well, I didn't impress him enough to get probation or that split sentence Mr. Beckett asked for." No. I believe it's approximately half, and I believe that a four-year sentence of 48 months is appropriate and reasonable, sufficient, and not greater than necessary.

And with that speech, Judge McCuskey announced my punishment for my actions. But he had a few more things to say. He recommended that I serve my sentence in a facility as close to my family in Central Illinois as possible. He added:

> It's further recommended that he serve his sentence in a facility that will allow him access to higher education opportunities and vocational training.

CHAPTER 32

> And, Scott, if only—if—I have no control of where they put you. So if they only put you in a facility with machinery that pays a few cents an hour, get out there and work on that machinery. Keep your brain working. Be with other people, and obviously help them. With your educational training, you can teach people also and help them while you're in prison.

I thought the judge was being awfully nice. I realized that he had still not belittled me like I had heard federal judges are known to do. He just sentenced me to four years but acknowledged that I could help others. He did not talk about my getting help or that I needed to get my life together.

He knew I was already doing that and advised me to stay the course.

Be a teacher to others. Make the best of my situation. Help other people like you always have.

Judge McCuskey continued. He said I did not have to pay a fine, but I would have five years of probation following my release. He read me a long list of terms I would have to follow while on probation.

One of the topics he discussed was when I would go to prison. Most defendants are taken into lockup right after court is adjourned. Judge McCuskey said this:

> The court does not believe that the evidence in this case shows the defendant to be a threat or danger to anyone. Because of this finding, the court will allow Scott Brown to self-report to the Bureau of Prisons on Wednesday, January 13, 2010, at 2:00 p.m. Moreover, because the defendant is not a danger to others or a risk of flight, the Court will recommend

to the Bureau of Prisons that the defendant be housed in a camp or minimum-security facility.

I fully expect that you'll get the designation of where you go between probation, your attorney, and the Bureau of Prisons, Scott. Because of this finding, I hope it does give you a better security clearance and hopefully a camp or minimum-security facility.

This sounded helpful. At least Judge McCuskey recommended that I go to the lowest possible level of prison. However, I would find out later that the Bureau of Prisons does not have to honor what the federal judge says.

Judge McCuskey continued by covering the rest of the items that would pay off the debt of my crime. He said I would be on probation for five years after I was released from prison. "During that time, you will not commit another federal, state, or local crime. I don't expect that." Again, he reaffirmed his belief that my breaking the law was a one-time thing.

He then said that while on my five-year probation, I should not have controlled substances in my possession. He followed this up by commenting that he does not expect that either, but he has to say that to everyone regardless of their history or crime.

The remaining rules of my probation were the general rules of submitting to DNA collection, refraining from the use of alcohol, participating in psychiatric services if needed, and not possessing a firearm.

The final part of his ruling was specific to my case. He stated that while on probation, I was not to receive or transmit sexually arousing material. He said that includes even popular magazines such as *Playboy*. He also talked about any computers I had. He said I would install filtering software on it to prevent access to sexually oriented websites.

CHAPTER 32

Further, I would allow any probation officer unannounced access to my computer. None of those rules mattered to me. I had followed them for almost two years already. Pornography was the vice that had caused the end of my first life. I had no desire to ever see it again.

The judge went on to say that I would not have "contact with any person under the age of 18 other than your two sons, except in the presence of a responsible adult who is aware of the nature of your background and current offense, and who has been approved by the Probation Office." Again, this did not matter to me. I had spent 14 years helping "persons under the age of 18." They would be fine without me. It was my sons I was worried about.

The judge finished his orders by saying I would need to register with the state sex offender registration agency in any state where I reside. I registered in Illinois a few days later.

The judge then asked the probation officer, federal prosecutor, and my attorney if he had left anything out or if they had anything further. My attorney asked for an extra month for me before reporting because I was still working on closing my mother's estate from her death a few months earlier. The judge granted that, and my new date to report was February 12, 2010.

There was nothing further to discuss. The judge ended my day in sentencing court by saying, "Good luck, Scott. You've got a lot of time left to continue to make important decisions to assist people and your special responsibility to society. I know you'll continue to help people in the future. You're free to go."

I never thought that Judge McCuskey was too hard on me. He is a federal judge appointed for life by the President of the United States—in this case, President Bill Clinton. Judge McCuskey is a man who respects the guidelines.

Congress sets the sentencing guidelines. Congress told the judges that my crime, with my circumstances, is worth eight to

10 years in prison. Judge McCuskey did something he had never done before. He gave me 50 percent of what Congress said was the restitution for my crime. I had hoped for mercy, and I received it.

I believe that if I had been arrested five years earlier when the guidelines for my crime were in the four-year range, Judge McCuskey would have given me a two-year sentence. He probably would have still determined that my actions were half as bad as someone searching and trading child pornography. The problem with this crime is that it is out of control. In response, Congress has raised the punishment for possession of child pornography almost every year for over a decade.

CHAPTER 33

After Judge McCuskey told me I was free to go, the courtroom came alive. My supporters filed out, and my attorney went over to talk to probation. I stood up to stretch my legs.

After a few moments, my attorney returned to our table and told me we would go to his office for a brief meeting. As I turned to walk out, I could not believe what I saw. The two Decatur police detectives had stopped the federal prosecutor. As I walked by, they had big smiles on their faces. One was aggressively shaking the prosecutor's hand. They said things like "great job" and "thank you." I immediately felt hate for them.

They had received what they wanted from day one. They wanted me in prison. They had won. They had no regard for the truth of what happened. They had spread rumors of what I might be, of all the children who would "come out of the woodwork." They were going to make sure I would never live in their neighborhood again, and my prison sentence would validate their version of the crime. At that moment, I almost asked them if they would be sure to play catch with my sons for the next few years. But Steve's words of wisdom came back to me. "Do not say one word."

I heard something a few weeks later that was ironic. I was talking to a member of my church who was friends with Detective Welker, the arresting detective. The church member had casually mentioned my case when he had bumped into the detective. He learned that the Decatur Police Department was not happy with the four-year sentence Judge McCuskey gave me. They wanted at least an eight-year sentence for what I had done. They also said my case would be the last one they would take before Judge McCuskey since he would just "make light of them." I think Judge McCuskey would be okay with that.

But today after the sentencing, they were there shaking hands with smiles on their faces, proudly telling the prosecutor "thank you" and "good job." That was the last time I would have to face any of my neighbors.

I walked past the prosecutor and out the back of the courtroom. In the hallway were about fifteen of my supporters, a few from my church and some parents of my former players. There were people I had taught and a few old friends. I thanked them for coming. I told them I had to go to the probation office and meet with my attorney. I promised to call them later with any new details. I was still in a state of semi-shock, trying to comprehend what had just happened. I left them there, some in tears, and went to take care of my business.

After a short meeting with the probation officer, I headed to Steve's office. I sat in his conference room with him, his assistant, and my brother Mark. Steve was visibly upset. He said he honestly thought we had a chance at probation but was now convinced without a doubt that Judge McCuskey will never give probation in one of these cases. Steve felt my case deserved it more than any case he had represented in all his years as an attorney.

We speculated as to which prison they would send me. Of course, we had no idea. But the judge clearly wanted me as close

CHAPTER 33

to my sons as possible. Since my home was in the center of Illinois, we were hoping I would go to the camp facility at Terre Haute, Indiana. That would only be a few hours away and would allow my sons to visit me.

Steve suggested I talk to some friends about bringing my sons to visit me, which would ease the burden on my ex-wife. He also told me that we could file a visitation order with the court to make sure I would get to see them. I reminded him that from the beginning of all this, my ex-wife had always wanted me to spend as much time as possible with my sons. I believed she would bring them to see me.

After about an hour, Mark and I left Steve's office. I spent the entire 45-minute ride home on the phone. The first person I called was my ex-wife. She was distraught that I was going away for four years and was concerned about our sons. I told her that when I came over that night to pick them up for visitation, we could sit down and talk to them. She agreed that would be a good idea. Later in the day, she called me back to let me know she had already talked to them. I was not okay with it, but what needed sharing had already been shared.

Reflection Section for Chapters 25-33 available on page 220

CHAPTER 34

Between the day I was sentenced and the day I had to report to prison, a few events occurred that I still remember as if they happened yesterday.

I had been trying to find someone to rent my mom's house while I was away. I called a friendly woman with whom I had taught. She had grown up in my neighborhood and said she was currently living in an apartment. After a 20-minute phone call, we arranged for her to walk through the house. Two days later, we agreed for her to rent it, and I had one less thing to handle.

For the last two months I was home, I spent two or three evenings a week and every weekend with my sons. My ex-wife always agreed for me to see them.

Usually I picked them up on Saturday. We did wood building projects at my shop and hung out at Menard's (that second happiest place on earth). We often went to the park. And in the evening, we ate pizza and watched a movie at my house. We played video games and threw the ball around in the yard. By nighttime, we were all pretty tired.

We decided to go back to our big church on Sunday mornings. I carefully manipulated the timing of our arrival and departure.

CHAPTER 34

I made sure we pulled into the parking lot as the service began. I wanted to go in the front door with my sons, turn the corner, and go straight up the stairs to the balcony where we had always sat as a family. I did not want to run into anyone who might know me.

The balcony was only big enough to hold about 25 people, but there were never more than five or 10 up there during the service. We were able to attend church without many people spotting us. I was embarrassed by what had happened and hoped to avoid being the "pew talk" of anyone there. I realized that just by being there I could distract some people from their worship time.

We always left the balcony during the last song, which allowed us to scoot out without too many people seeing us. I never told my sons why we did that.

Even in the small group of "balcony people," reactions from others were mixed. A few would say hello to us every week, and others would only glance at us and then turn away. I don't think my sons ever noticed. But I could attend church services with my sons, which was the main point. I did not know whether their mom would take them to church after I left.

I remember another time when I stopped to see my pastor, Wray, for some counseling. During the conversation, he asked if I had considered sharing my story with the congregation. He knew I had been talking to as many men as possible about my case. I wanted everyone I had the chance to influence to understand the dangers of pornography addiction, especially on the Internet with file sharing programs.

Wray told me that since my case had hit the news, other men had been talking to him about their own struggles with pornography. But he knew that some men would never come forward, and they also needed to hear the message. I agreed to start working on what our church calls "My Personal Sharing" message.

Wray met with the church's elders to see what they thought of my presenting a message in front of the church. They decided I could come in and record my message by video to be shown after I left for prison.

I found out later that the elders were concerned that I might offend some people. Pornography is a touchy topic, so I understood I would refer to what happened as "downloading illegal videos."

Just as importantly, the elders were concerned that I might offend some specific people. One of the members of our church who attended regularly and sat right up front was the State Attorney who was initially in charge of prosecuting my case before it went to federal court. The elders were concerned about how personal my "personal sharing" might get.

I worked on my presentation by following Wray's advice. He told me that before I started writing, I should pray for God's guidance. After all, I was going to be speaking in His house. I followed this advice and completed my message in just two evenings.

The following week I had a meeting to read it to Pastor Wray. I read it to him through tears. If I was going to do this as a presentation, I was going to need to be able to get through it dry-eyed. When I finished talking, I looked up at Pastor Wray. He, too, had tears in his eyes. He gave me a big hug and thanked me.

I remember telling him my fear. I was worried that people would give me no respect and would not listen to me because of my crime. He told me that my talk would have just the opposite effect.

He explained that when he speaks about addictions to various things, he is talking as an outsider. He has never been through them himself, and the congregation knows that. I, however, was going to be a strong influence. I was someone who had hit rock bottom on an issue that was growing out of control in America. My words would come from firsthand experience. After hearing my speech, Wray knew it would impact people.

CHAPTER 34

We decided I would come in to record the video a few days before I was scheduled to leave. I took this very seriously and genuinely hoped to help others. I practiced reading my eight-minute presentation over and over. But I always had tears in my eyes somewhere during the reading. Sometimes I stopped in the middle and broke down uncontrollably. I needed to get through my talk calmly and clearly to convey the importance of the message.

The day to share my story came. I showed up at the church, and Wray said the video production guy was waiting for us. He had set up his camera and had it aimed at the pulpit. I put my speech down, and after taking a few deep breaths, I began:

> I am here today to share information about my life, the blessings God gave me, and how my weaknesses took away many of those blessings.
>
> And I hope to be an example.
>
> For those of you that don't know me, I'm Scott Brown. I have been a member here at St. Paul's for about 15 years. My boys and I occupy seat numbers 3, 4, and 5 in the balcony under the pipes. I know we don't have assigned seats here at St. Paul's, but you know how it is.
>
> This personal sharing might be the hardest thing I have done in a long time, but here it goes. I grew up in Decatur and attended St. John's and St. Paul's Lutheran Schools. I was a product of a dad who left when I was five. To my memory, I was the only kid in my class who did not have both parents at home.
>
> How times have changed. I never missed a church service on Sunday until I was about 14 years old, old enough to tell my mom I was not going, and

she was not big enough to make me. In my young life, my friend's dads were the most positive things I had.

I remember them taking me to Indian Guides, Boy Scouts, and other father-son events. But my entire childhood, I wanted a regular family, which carried into my adult life.

After high school, I worked for six years before going to college. In 1994, I graduated from Eastern Illinois University with degrees in teaching physical education, history, and science.

Shortly after that, I married my girlfriend of eight years and became a teacher and very successful coach. About that same time, I came to St. Paul's. I did the basics class and became a member in front of the congregation. You all clapped for me. Thank you.

In 2007, I had what I had always wanted—a successful teaching and coaching career, a home in a nice neighborhood, a nice truck—and I had just started a business to supplement my teaching career. Most importantly, I had a family—a great wife of 14 years and two wonderful sons. I brought my family to church almost every week. God had blessed me way more than I deserved.

My entire life changed two years ago. On July 17, 2008, seven police cars showed up at my house, and I was arrested for possession of illegal videos on my computer. Many stories came out about what happened. I was plastered on the front page of our local paper. I was on the television news as the main story.

CHAPTER 34

This was the end for my family and the best years of my life. The night I was arrested, I explained to the detective that I had been downloading adult videos on the Internet on and off for about five years. My online searches produced all kinds of videos, sometimes ones I did not want, including illegal videos. When these unwanted videos came to my computer, I attempted to delete them. But as it turned out, I was not successful. I never had any intentions of having illegal videos on my computer. This is not the story that made it to the newspaper or television news.

It took almost two years for the truth to finally come out in the federal courthouse on December 4th. After all rumors were put to rest, what I told the detectives that first night turned out to be the truth, but I had no choice but to plead guilty to possessing the illegal videos. At my sentencing, the judge said things I had waited almost two years to hear.

The federal judge stated that my case should never have been sent to federal court. He complimented me for telling the truth to the detective on the night I was arrested and for continuing to tell the truth about what happened throughout the entire process. He complimented me for leading an exemplary life and helping children in the school system for the last 14 years. And he said, "Scott, I do not believe you are a criminal, you never were a criminal, and you never will be a criminal."

Then he said the most unbelievable thing. He said I would spend the next 48 months in federal prison starting February 12th and that I would be an example to others. His exact words were, "If someone like Mr. Brown can go to jail for this, then it should send a message that anyone can go to jail for this." No message will be sent if I do not speak to you today. My mistake will not be an example, and my going away will be a waste of time. My life will be a waste of time, and I will be forgotten.

The day after I was arrested, I came to see pastor Wray. I explained that I could no longer come to St. Paul's because with all the news coverage, I would be a distraction for those who came here to worship. I found a home at Pastor Troy's house church, which was less like a church and more like a Bible study to me. And in my previous 41 years, I never went to an actual Bible study. I came here, I sat here, and I left here. I once heard a pastor on TV talking about how the Word sits on some people like water on the sidewalk in the summer. That was me, the five-minute Christian.

I could listen to a sermon about hatred and forgiveness but then go home and forget it when the baseball coach did not play my son in the game. I could listen to a sermon on reading your Bible daily and really get into the Word, and then do nothing but show up next Sunday because that is what I did as a passive Christian. I could listen to a sermon on respecting your spouse and not looking at others with lust and then go home and watch adult videos that night. I remember Pastor Wray preaching on pornography, sitting in seat #4 in the balcony, and thought it did not apply to me because I was following some of the other parts of the Bible. I

CHAPTER 34

chose only to follow the Bible verses I wanted. I have learned the hard way that if the Word does not soak into your life, if you are not constantly on guard, Satan will find your weaknesses and use them against you. Sin grows.

I believe God has a plan for each of us, but it is up to us to follow it. In our lives, there are Ys in the road. One leg of the road takes you to where God wants and expects you to be, and the other takes you to where Satan laughs at you. The good news about our God is that when you go down the wrong path and realize it, you can turn around, and God is waving you back to the correct way.

I am not a better Christian than I was two years ago. I am a different Christian. Today, I have two issues I struggle with on a Christian level.

First is forgiveness. I do not know how I will ever forgive myself for my absolute carelessness and the pain my sons will go through in the next four years. There are verses in the Bible saying you should forgive each other. If the Lord can forgive us for everything we do, how can we not forgive each other? I will never ask my sons to forgive me.

My second struggle is anger. I am angry at what I felt was unfair treatment being sent to the federal court system where prison time is certain, while others who do equal or even worse crimes are treated differently. I am not trying to place blame or declare innocence, but I am angry when I try to make sense of it all. I am angry that I did not make my marriage strong enough to stand against divorce in the face of this tragedy. We all get married, for better or worse, in front of God. The better is the fun part; the worse is the opportunity to grow—the opportunity to teach your children about commitment. If my family could have survived this, we could have survived anything. And what would that have taught my sons about commitment and family?

Unfortunately, in America, families are expendable and replaceable. I am not angry with my ex-wife. I still love her very much, but I am upset that my boys are one more casualty of divorce.

I have had two painful years. The results of my carelessness have cost me my career and passion. I loved teaching. I feel like it is what I was meant to do. My actions have cost me my marriage of 14 years. I loved my wife and our family more than anything. I was looking forward to having the kind of marriage my friends' parents had.

Most importantly, my conduct has damaged my two young sons. I love my two sons more than anything in this world. I grew up without a father, and I never wanted my boys to grow up without a father in their lives. I can only pray that God helps me live above my frustration and anger over this situation.

I want to thank Pastors Wray, Rob, and Troy for counseling me these past few years. I also thank all my close friends from Pastor Troy's Bible studies, Eric Brie's family for being my neighbor even after I had to move out of our home, and Jan Allen for never once looking at me with judgment when I came for an appointment here.

CHAPTER 34

> I am sharing with you today in the hope that I may help prevent someone else from going through the same pain I am going through. It does not have to be the same weakness that I had. Satan is not picky. He can knock you out with over-drinking, drugs, gambling, dishonesty, stealing, and other sins.
>
> Someone here today might be near the edge of ruining their family. I hope you don't. And please do not think that it can't happen to you. I would ask all of you today, are you doing anything at all that might hamper your relationship with your family, even that one little thing that might be okay because you follow the rest of the Bible? You would be surprised how fast sin can grow if you let it.
>
> In closing, I would ask the family men here—sometime soon, send your wife some flowers for no reason. Play a game with your children, and let them win. And bring your family to church every week.
>
> And if it is crowded, it's okay to use seats 3, 4, and 5 in the balcony.

I made it through my speech with dry eyes. The video production man was not so lucky. Right after he turned the camera off, he walked to the back of the church in tears. Wray told me how it touched him was how it would reach other men.

The week after I reported to federal prison, I called Pastor Wray. He told me that the elders had previewed the video and agreed it needed to be shared with the congregation. He included that many of the elders were very touched by my words. It was to be shown the following Sunday at all three services.

I called Pastor Wray the following week to check in. He said that over 800 members had been at the services on Sunday, and "there was not a dry eye in the place." My question was whether or not the sharing of my story would make a lasting impact. He thought it would and said he had many people contact him regarding putting it on the church website so others could view it. That, however, was not going to happen.

It turns out that Monday morning, after showing the video in church, Pastor Wray received a phone call from the State Attorney. He and one of his prosecutors were concerned that it made them look bad.

When Wray told me this, I was disappointed. Three times in my speech, I expressed that my fall was totally my fault. I did not blame anyone else. I was guilty of possession. The purpose of the entire presentation was to keep other men from losing their families. It was to bring awareness to other men and encourage them to cherish what God had given them. But the state attorney's primary concern, the only thing he had gotten out of my eight-minute message, was that I had made the prosecutors look bad.

Let me take this moment to say that was not my intention. I could not help how they felt. I am sorry the prosecutors did not get the genuine message of my heartfelt presentation. Sometimes pride can work as a blinder.

CHAPTER 35

One of the other events I remember very clearly before I had to report to prison was the day I got the letter informing me which prison I would be reporting to. I had been anxiously checking the mail every day. About a month after my sentencing, the letter arrived.

I opened the letter and quickly read the page. It was a short letter of just a few lines. It stated that I would report to the federal prison in Forrest City, Arkansas, and be housed in the low-level facility. I immediately turned on my computer to see precisely where Forrest City, Arkansas, was.

I found out that Forrest City is about a seven-hour drive from my house. I was distraught. I knew the judge specifically stated that I should be sent somewhere as close to home as possible. I could not imagine that seven hours from my sons was the closest facility possible.

I had done some checking and knew there was a prison in Terre Haute, Indiana, just two hours from home. At that distance, I was sure church friends would bring my sons there once a month or so. But seven hours one way? That was not good.

I got on the phone with my attorney and told him what the letter said. He was also upset but reminded me that the judge does not give orders to the Bureau of Prisons (BOP). He only makes suggestions. He confirmed that I would have to report to Forrest City, but I might be able to transfer later.

While talking with Steve, I asked him about the low-level designation. The judge had requested that I get a placement at a minimum-security prison. Again, Steve reminded me that the judge could only make suggestions to the BOP.

As it turns out, Forrest City, Arkansas, is the closest federal prison to my home that is designated as a low-security facility. I would later find out that no one guilty of my crime was allowed to go to a minimum-security prison—ever. The BOP labels us with a Public Safety Factor, or PSF.

A low-security prison is the best you can do if you are considered a danger to the public. Under BOP policy, regardless of the court findings, the determination of the government's psychologist, and the specific circumstances of my crime, I am now considered a danger to the public.

After hanging up the phone with Steve, I called my ex-wife. I explained what the letter said, and she was not happy either. She did not want to have to bring the boys seven hours one way to see me in prison.

I called a few of my friends from church, and they were very supportive. They assured me that it would not be a big deal. They would make a weekend of it, drive down on a Friday after work with my sons, and stay the night. Then they would visit me the next day. It sounded so easy, but it would never happen. My ex-wife was uncomfortable with other people taking our boys on an overnight trip.

Less than a year after I reported to Forrest City, she and the boys moved to Florida. I would not see my sons for four years.

CHAPTER 36

Another vivid memory was my last evening with my sons before I had to report to prison. I picked them up after school. We went to eat and then went back to what had been my mother's house. I had been moving my possessions to the basement. The new renter had agreed to let me use an area in the basement to store my stuff while I was gone. The boys helped me carry some items downstairs, and then we looked at games we used to play. After a while, we went outside and played catch with the football and kicked the soccer ball around. When it came time for them to leave, we piled into the truck and drove back to the family home.

I spent most of the 15-minute drive making small talk with my sons. It was starting to settle in that this would be our last ride together for quite some time.

As we stopped in the driveway, my older son grabbed onto me and gave me a big hug. We were both crying. I kept telling him how sorry I was. He told me he was going to go inside and get Mom. He wanted her to say goodbye to me.

Both of them walked out of the house within a minute. My ex-wife and I looked at each other for a moment. What came back to me was that we had met when she was 18 years old. We had known each other for over 20 years. She was the love of my life. I asked myself why this had to happen. It was not fair.

I asked permission to hug her, and she allowed it. We hugged for a moment, and I told her I was sorry for what seemed like the thousandth time. For almost two years I had ended nearly every conversation we had with those same words.

My ex-wife said, "It's okay" and turned to walk back into the house. My older son came over and grabbed me around the waist. I picked him up and held him. Eventually, I told him it was time for him to go. Being the "big boy," he wiped the tears from his eyes and walked into the garage and up the three steps to the entry door. The screen door shut behind him, and he turned around to look at me. He put up one hand and briefly waved. With that, he moved away from the door, which was the last time I would see him for four years.

This whole time, my younger son who was now 10 years old had been sitting in the truck. It was now his turn to say goodbye. I climbed into the front seat next to him. He was motionless, just like when I said goodbye to him before they left for Louisiana. However, this time he had tears rolling down both cheeks.

I only got out his name before he turned and grabbed me. He began crying out loud. His grip on me was an effort to keep me there and not allow me to leave. I let him hold on for as long as he wanted.

We sat in the truck hugging each other for several minutes. Eventually, our breathing slowed, and our tears stopped flowing. I told him it was time to go. We both got out of the truck, and I held his hand. We walked toward the garage and gave each other a final big hug. I remember telling him that I loved him, that God would watch over us, and that I would see him soon.

The goodbye could have been the ending of a sad movie. His little legs took him to the three steps to go into the house.

CHAPTER 36

He climbed to the top and put his hand on the button to close the big garage door. I had gotten back into the truck and was watching through the windshield. He pushed the button to let the garage door shut and waved sadly. We watched each other until the door was too low for us to see each other. That was my last image of him.

I drove back to my house, crying all the way. I yelled to God about why this had to happen this way. I asked Him to take care of my sons. That evening was the lowest time of my entire life so far. There would only be one that was worse and would come almost six months later while I was in prison.

When I got back to my house, I called my ex-wife. She told me that both boys had been crying, and she was having them get ready for bed. She was considering letting them stay home from school the next day. But we finally agreed that they should go. It would help take their minds off of what was going on.

I asked to talk to the boys so we could say prayers. Our prayers that night were filled with words about keeping everyone safe while I was gone. Both of my sons understood that God is in control. I now realize that they understood this better than I did then. They still had the childlike faith that seems to get screwed up as we get older.

CHAPTER 37

After I hung up the phone with my sons, I continued to prepare to leave the next day. It was about 9:00 p.m., and I worked until about 2:00 a.m. putting the rest of my stuff in the basement. I awoke at about 6:00 a.m. to finish cleaning the house. My drive to federal prison in Forrest City, Arkansas, would take me seven hours away from home and my sons.

This day was also memorable. I took care of a few loose ends, put checks in the mail for bills, and dropped off some valuables at a friend's house. It was the end of that life.

I had rented a car for the trip, and a couple of my friends agreed to go with me and bring the vehicle back. I was to report by 2:00 p.m. on Friday. We decided to leave on Thursday and stay the night in a hotel near the prison. I did not want to go, but since I had to, I did not want to be late.

On our way out of town, we stopped at our church. Two other friends met us there. I wanted to see the video where I shared my story, and they were anxious to see it too. The youth pastor, my friend who had lived across the street from our family home, had set up a room for us to preview it.

The six of us viewed the video together. It was hard for me to watch now that the time had come to leave. My self-inflicted chaos

CHAPTER 37

had been going on for almost two years, and reality was setting in. We all shared a tearful goodbye. And with that, we left the church and headed for my temporary home in Arkansas.

CHAPTER 38

We pulled into the prison parking lot at 1:00 p.m. on February 12, 2010. I had showed up a little early to check things out. Forrest City is known as a prison complex since there are three security facilities there—a minimum security facility (or camp), the low-security facility I was reporting to, and a medium security facility.

We sat in the car for a few minutes, looking at the scene. The outside of the main low-security building was all concrete and block. Ten-foot-high fences branched out in both directions for a couple hundred yards. Behind the main building were three large buildings for housing the inmates.

There was a gigantic courtyard with sidewalks leading to the main building and the housing units. To one side of the housing units was the recreation yard. A large dirt running track surrounded a soccer field, two baseball fields, four basketball courts, and other game areas and activities. After taking it all in, I knew it was time to enter the front door. We did not make it halfway there before armed guards stopped us.

We were about 50 feet from the rental car when two trucks pulled up to the front door and a white van parked at the end of

CHAPTER 38

the sidewalk about 75 feet away. Guards with shotguns climbed out and yelled at us to go stand by our car. We went quickly.

The front doors opened, and out came two prisoners. Each was handcuffed, and the cuffs were attached to the waist with a chain. Both prisoners wore ankle shackles. These "leg handcuffs" allowed the prisoners to shuffle toward the van, but that was the most they would do. As they made their way toward the van, two guards, one for each of them, walked behind each prisoner and held the chain that was attached to the prisoner's waist.

I had been so shocked at the security measures that I did not even notice at first that there were two more guards by the van. One was the driver, and the other was the van escort armed with a pistol.

To load these two prisoners into the waiting van required full shackles and six guards armed with two shotguns and a pistol. It also took two security trucks, a transport van, and an escort vehicle.

I looked at the sign on the building to make sure we were at the low-security facility. We were. I had wondered where they were taking these two and what they had done to warrant such security measures. I also realized that these were the types of guys I would be living with for the next four years.

I found out later that these two guys were going out on a simple medical run. They needed medical attention that was unavailable at the prison. They had not committed some unthinkable violent crime in prison. They were just injured or sick.

After the vehicles pulled away with these two criminals, one of the shotgun guards told us it was okay to come to the front door. I was very anxious at that point.

The three of us entered a pleasant enough lobby with a metal detector next to a reception desk. I told the lady there that I was to report at 2:00 p.m. She pointed us to the waiting area. My two friends and I went there and sat down.

One of my friends, Guy, suggested we say a prayer. We were all still a little shaken by the production outside. Guy led us in prayer, asking for my safety, and we talked about nothing specific for a few minutes. Then a female officer came over and announced that they were ready for me. She told me to leave my wallet, watch, and any other personal belongings with my friends so they could take them home. She explained that I would be issued clothes, and they would mail my clothes home.

I had my Bible with me and asked if I could bring it in. She told me it would be up to the officer who would process me into the prison. I hugged my friends and said goodbye. I was led behind the reception area, and the solid steel door slammed behind me. My time in the custody of the Federal Bureau of Prisons had begun.

CHAPTER 39

The person processing me flipped through my Bible. She explained that some people stash drugs or other items in their Bibles. While investigating, she warned that if she found something illegal, it would be an additional crime, and I could be given more prison time.

After thoroughly checking for contraband, she agreed that I could take my Bible with me into the prison. But she let me know that not all the officers would allow it, and I was lucky she was working on that day. At that point in my life, I did not feel very lucky.

She handed me my Bible and directed me to wait in the holding cell across from the processing area. I was there for about 20 minutes. I just sat on the bench and thought about my sons. Eventually, a rather imposing male officer opened the door.

I followed him to the changing area. There I had to strip off all my clothes. I was handed a pair of boxer shorts, socks, shoes, and a one-piece white jumpsuit. The white socks were paper thin, and the shoes were simple slippers. My personal clothes and shoes were boxed up in front of me and sealed in a shipping box to be sent home. I now officially had nothing of my own except for my Bible.

My next step was to visit the psychologist. I entered her office and sat down. She only wanted to know if I felt like killing myself. I explained that I had some anxiety, but as I told probation almost two years earlier, I would never kill myself because I had two sons at home. I may have been absent now, but I would be home in four years.

The psychologist was satisfied with my answer. She then asked me if I would like to be prescribed some drugs for my anxiety. She claimed the medication would help me sleep better. I declined since I never wanted to put drugs in my body unless it was absolutely necessary. Other inmates later told me I should have said yes to the drugs. I could have sold them for money if I did not want them. That thought did not cross my mind at that moment.

I had to visit a nurse briefly after that. She asked me about my medical history and drew some blood. I had one stop left. A correctional officer (CO) wanted to speak with me.

He led me to a small office with a simple desk. He introduced himself and told me that he knew why I was there. He had looked at my charge and needed to talk to me "for my safety." I was all ears.

He warned me that other prisoners view my crime as the worst crime. I was and would be part of a group of men who were not accepted. He explained that a few years ago, it was common for inmates with my crime to be attacked and beaten by some of the others. He also told me that I probably did not need to worry about the black or Hispanic guys; those groups did not care why a white guy like me was there. He advised me that this had been a problem with the white guys. But he believed this was in the past because they had had several meetings to deal with the issue. He then suggested that when I get to my unit, I lie.

He told me that most likely, as soon as I got in there, someone would come up and introduce himself. They would want to know why I was there. He told me it would be best to tell the other

CHAPTER 39

prisoners that I was there on a drug case and not say what I had been admitting since day one.

I decided to give the officer a quick explanation of my case. He told me that the details would not matter to the other prisoners. I expressed that the problem with saying I was there because of drugs was that I did not know about any drugs other than smoking marijuana 20 years ago. I told the CO that there was no way I could fake a drug conviction. He had me worried, though. I asked him what other kind of crime might be believable.

He told me to try mail fraud or bank fraud. I was aware of what bank fraud was. We created the story that I had taken out multiple home loans on the same piece of property. Then I used the cash for a few trips and vehicles. He assured me it would be enough to get me locked up at this low facility. So with that knowledge, he led me to the door that would lead out onto the compound.

As he opened the steel door, I saw that the three large buildings for housing stood across a large area with sidewalks. Before I walked out, he handed me my bed roll that contained sheets, a blanket, and some toiletries.

He pointed to the building on the left and told me to go up the left stairs to the unit on top. Each of the three two-story buildings was divided into four housing units. I stepped out, and he said, "You will be fine. Good luck."

I thought to myself, *If I will be fine, then why do I need luck?*

The steel door closed behind me, and with my new possessions tucked under my arm, I walked the long sidewalk to the building on the left. I opened another steel door at the top of the stairs and entered. It was not what I had expected.

There were no bars. There were no cells. The unit reminded me of the office area at the newspaper company where I once worked with half-wall dividers to give everyone their space.

These cubicles had concrete block walls just under six feet high to divide each cell. The cubes ran all the way to the back of the unit. In front of the first set of cubicles was what everyone called skid row. Four sets of bunk beds were separated by two lockers, each with no walls dividing them. The least private area in the house, it contained the most undesirable beds. And it was where they put all the new arrivals.

I walked into the unit, and everyone who could see me was looking at me. New arrivals are a big deal. Inmates want to know as soon as possible if you might fit into their group.

I also noticed that nobody else was wearing my white jumpsuit. Everyone was dressed in either gray sweat suits, T-shirts, or khaki-colored pants and shirts. I was already sticking out like a sore thumb.

As I stood inside the front door, obviously unsure where to go, someone yelled for me to turn to my right and go to the office. That is what I did.

The CO in the office was a young black woman. She was busy doing something on her computer. She looked up at me and asked with irritation, "What do you need?"

I told her I had just reported. She told me to put my stuff on the first empty bunk on skid row and find a blue mattress. Great directions.

I left her office and went to the corner bunk closest to the steel door where I entered. I observed that all the other bunks had blue mattresses under the sheets. I put my stuff on the top empty metal bunk.

A few inmates were walking around, and others were sitting on their bunks. Some were observing me from their cubes. Only one person said anything to me. I was looking around the area for some sort of blue mattress but was not going to make eye contact with anyone just yet. After a few moments, I realized I did not

CHAPTER 39

have the courage to walk around and look for the mattress. I had no idea where to look. This was not my home as it was to everyone else. I was the new guy, so I walked back to the CO's office.

When I got to her door, she was still looking at something on the computer. I told her I could not find a blue mattress. She exaggerated a sigh, stood up, walked past me, and muttered, "Come on."

She in her blue uniform and I in my white jumpsuit walked down the hallway to the end of the unit. There were cubicles on each side of us. She was looking right and left at each one. We turned right when we reached the end and walked the short 30-foot space behind the last cube. That was when I realized another set of cubes was on the other side of this unit. We were walking a big loop. Picture a square racetrack with cubicles on the infield, back-to-back facing out, and more cubicles where the stands would be facing inward. We turned right again and walked all the way back down the other hall toward the front of the unit again. I had just been given the grand tour.

I noticed very early in the procession that as we neared any cube, the men stopped what they were doing and looked at her and at me. They had learned to see what was going on when they heard the jingle of a CO's keys. It was evident to them that I was new. I was very uncomfortable with all the staring.

We went back to the front of the unit near skid row, and the CO said something about needing to go in the back to get a mattress. We walked past her office and through some other doors to a storage room and retrieved the elusive blue mattress. We walked back out, and she returned to her office. I proceeded to my bunk, and I was on my own. Her responsibility to me was done for now.

I made my bed and was sitting on top in my white monkey suit, trying to read the prison manual I had received earlier. But

I could not concentrate. I was aware from the time I started to make my bed that I was being watched.

Two bunks over, a large black man stared at me. I must be clear that when I say large, I do not mean fat. This man was probably about 50 years old, a little over 6 feet tall, and must have weighed a solid 230 pounds. He was just sitting there sipping his coffee and staring at me. I wondered how long it would be before something happened.

After about five minutes of trying to concentrate on the manual, I heard this big man's voice. Still staring at me, he roared, "Hey, new guy!"

I looked at him. My heart jumped and was beating a mile a minute. I realized that if he came at me, my only option would be to jump off the far side of the bunk and either head down the long hall or toward the CO's office. I replied to him with the only word I could, and I believe my voice cracked like when I was 13 years old. I simply said, "Yeah?"

I soon learned his name—Mr. Hall. He held up his coffee mug and said, "You want some coffee?"

I exhaled as I replied, "No, thanks."

CHAPTER 40

Over the few years Mr. Hall and I lived in the same unit, he became my ally. We only discussed why he was in prison a few times. He had been into drugs, had threatened a witness, and had been branded a career criminal by the BOP. He was initially housed at a higher security prison but had worked his way down over the years through good behavior.

Many inmates devote themselves to something while they are locked up. Attempting to pass the time quickly, they try to stay busy. If you just lie around in your bunk all the time, the clock moves very slowly.

At his previous prisons, Mr. Hall had gotten into weightlifting. If you ever catch a television show about prisons, they often show the fitness area with all the big guys standing around one massive guy who bench presses something equal to a small car. That was Mr. Hall—the bench press guy.

One evening during my first winter, I found Mr. Hall doing arm curls with the work he did in the laundry room. He curled a large cloth bag filled about three feet high with paper. He had tied the bag to a small broomstick as a handle. He asked me if I wanted to join him, so I did.

I should describe my stature. I am 6 feet tall and weighed about 190 pounds at the time. I had worked out during my life, but I was not made of muscle. One time during our workout, Mr. Hall brought in a cloth tape measure he had made. It was to check the circumference of his arms. For fun, we also checked mine.

We discovered that my 13-inch biceps were the same size as his forearm. His biceps measured just over 20 inches. He was my workout partner. We were a funny combination, but it worked.

Mr. Hall was the first inmate to really talk to me upon my arrival on skid row. But there were others too. As I sat there reading, others came up and introduced themselves. I would later find out that some of these guys just introduced themselves so they could get my name and find out where I was from. Many alliances were built just because you were from a particular state. I'm from Illinois, so I did not have many home boys there in Arkansas.

But other guys introduced themselves because they wanted to help if they could. They had also been new to the prison system at one time.

I reported on a Friday. Monday was going to be a holiday. So that left me in my monkey suit and slippers for three and a half days.

I should mention that I was the only new guy who reported on that particular day, which meant I was the only one wearing a white jumpsuit among 1,800 inmates. Everyone else was in dark gray or khaki.

One of the men who introduced himself was Tim. He, in turn, introduced me to a few others. They all pitched in and donated a pair of sweatpants, a shirt, some shoes, and some regular socks and underwear. I felt relieved because now I could look like everyone else as I figured this place out.

I was also given shower shoes and other adult-sized toiletries, not the sample sizes. They also gave me a drinking mug and a few cans of Pepsi. Tim asked me if I wanted anything to eat. He had a

CHAPTER 40

locker full of food—candy, noodles, chili, and all kinds of snacks. I was not hungry at the time, but I was given various items over the next four days.

At first, I was cautious about receiving anything from anyone. The CO who talked to me when I reported warned me not to accept anything of value from the other inmates. He explained to me that "nothing is free."

He told me someone might give me $10 worth of stuff today, but once I had money on my account and could go to the commissary, they would expect $20 or more worth of things in return. So why did I accept this help from Tim and go against the CO's advice? One reason: Tim's explanation.

After Tim brought a few things to me, I asked him what he would want in return. He said, "Nothing." He explained that a lot of the inmates go to the chapel services. Outside of prison, they'd be able to put money in a collection plate each week. They could not do that here. Instead, they gave what they could to those in need without expecting anything in return.

This was not a new idea to me, this giving to those in need. But it was not what I expected to find in prison. I was among criminals—evil people, law breakers, people who would hurt others for no reason. I had seen the television specials. I thought I knew about this place before I arrived here. As it turned out, I did not.

CHAPTER 41

Over my three-plus years at this low-security prison, I learned that the facility housed people who are lifelong criminals. They have done some awful things in their lives. Some have hurt countless people. But they have served their time at higher security prisons and have worked their way down to this more trusting place.

The majority of men were there simply because they had a drug problem. They were either caught using illegal drugs, they sold drugs to make enough money to feed their habit, or they didn't use but sold drugs to make a living.

Some guys committed crimes that got them labeled sexual offenders. It is the second-largest population segment but also the fastest growing one. Given my unintentional possession of child pornography, I became part of that population. Men convicted of that charge are considered the lowest of the low, and many have the most challenging time in prison.

While at Forrest City Low, I met all kinds of people, some habitual liars. I will never forget one guy who told me he had worked for my dad. I had previously mentioned that my dad was a Realtor in Florida. This guy insisted he had cleaned up some houses my dad had listed. I resisted asking the guy to describe my

CHAPTER 41

dad. He was so excited to tell me about our connection that I did not want to break his bubble.

I saw celebrities. We had a very famous rap artist and actor there. I will never forget the first time he made an appearance in the recreation yard. There was a line of over 100 inmates waiting to talk to him. Many of them just wanted to share their own rapping skills.

I also experienced the joy of meeting a former professional football player who had won a Super Bowl ring with the Dallas Cowboys. I first met him when we were on opposing debate teams at the prison. We continued to speak to each other while doing time together. We usually ran into each other during the Sunday morning Christian church service at the chapel.

Some of the guys I met were hard-core criminals. I talked to one guy who had been locked up for over 20 years for drugs. He came to prison when he was just in his early 20s. He was leaving as a man over 40 years old. I will never forget two things about him—the excitement he had the night before he left and the look on his face eight months later when he returned for violating his probation.

There were men of all ages housed with me. The oldest of our inmates were the ones who amazed me the most. "Ralph" was 72 years old. He walked in the front door one day to report for his one-year federal sentence. He had been a lifelong gun collector. After 72 years of life, he had broken a federal law. He was at a gun show and unknowingly bought a gun that was somehow illegal. It was not some rocket launcher; it was a simple firearm with an altered barrel. He, like most people, assumed that if it was for sale at a professionally run show, it was legal. Federal agents were at the gun show peddling the guns to catch a few criminals.

Ralph told me that the worst part of his one-year prison sentence was that as a felon, he was no longer able to own a firearm. He was forced to sell his prized gun collection. He had never been arrested before.

I was also housed with the very young. Seeing "kids" come through the door always broke my heart. Some of those inmates were barely 18 years old. They always looked lost when they arrived.

When I think of the younger inmates, two individuals come to mind. Both of them had similar cases. They were both caught up in drug manufacturing or selling at a young age. One was in his early 20s with a 20-year sentence. The other was in his early 30s with 16 years to go.

I think of the hope I had in my first life 20 years ago. I think about all I was able to accomplish in my previous 16 years, all the people, especially students, I was able to help and guide. And I realize that neither of those guys will be able to enjoy finding a wife, creating a family, and growing as a person as I was able to do.

I served just over three years in prison during this middle part of my life. Due to my life experience, I am well on the road to recovery. But I wonder how those two younger guys will ever recover from such devastating sentences at such young ages. I question if there was no other penalty that could have been given to them other than 20 years in prison to pay for their mistakes at a young age. Their cases are the hardest for me to accept.

CHAPTER 42

Along with all the hard-core criminals and young and old inmates I met, there is also a particular group of men from whom I've been able to learn. The Forrest City federal prison contained some of the finest, God-fearing, people-loving, brother-helping men I've ever met.

While in prison, I met a few genuine, faithful Christians. I also met many men who were searching for Christ and some pretend Christians. The spiritual reality there is very similar to what you find in the free world. When I arrived at the prison, I did not know the difference between these groups. But I soon realized I had been a pretend Christian.

The term *Christian* does not mean someone who believes in Christ. It means someone who follows Christ. A Christian is someone who is saved, someone who has accepted the salvation offered as a free gift of God, someone who is walking in the Light every day.

For 43 years, I only believed in Christ, that He probably lived at some point in the past. He was merely my insurance policy, and I was really not a Christian.

It was not until I came to prison that I could focus on the most important thing about life. The most important thing about life is to prepare for what will happen to you when you die. Prison allowed me the time I needed to study God's Word. Through that and prayer, I accepted God's love, grace, and mercy for me.

Before my time in prison, I had too many important things going on in my life to focus on what would happen after I died. I was a very successful teacher and coach. I was blessed with a loving wife and, in my humble and unbiased opinion, the best two sons on the entire planet. I had a new house and a nice truck. I was living the American dream. But then I went to prison. And in prison I had only one possession in my life—my Bible. I could only bring my Bible thanks to the providence of having the correct guard process me.

Shortly after my arrest, I began talking to my pastor every week. I also talked daily to some of my friends who were church members. That sort of behavior is what most humans do when they get into trouble. If we have some religion in our background, we turn to it when things in our foreground have been taken away.

When I walked in the door of the prison housing unit on that Friday, a few of the Christians spotted my Bible. By noon on Saturday, they had told me about the chapel and all the different religious services. I assured them that I was a Christian (I was not yet) and that I would attend services on Sunday.

Someone suggested that I request some correspondent Bible studies. I jumped in with both feet and sent away for about 15 studies.

Sunday morning I rose early and headed over to the chapel. I discovered that Sunday service in the Forrest City Arkansas Federal Prison differs from a Sunday Lutheran service in central Illinois. I grew up with pastors who spoke gently to the

CHAPTER 42

congregation. They delivered the message with care and thought and asked us to apply it to our daily lives.

The first Sunday service I attended in Arkansas was heavily Southern Baptist. During that service I was not "asked" to apply anything. I was "told" via a loud voice and a lot of finger-pointing from the pulpit to apply Christ to my life. There, in Forrest City Low, I had entered a different religious world. I had never seen a preacher jump up and down before during a sermon.

I remember my reaction after one of the first services I attended. I told one of the guys in my unit that I did not get anything out of the service. I had sat in the chapel for an hour and listened to the chaplain scream about how I could be better and not have to do the same old things, how it was time to change my life and allow Christ to work in my heart.

I explained to him that I had already changed my life after I got arrested. I told him I did not need to hear that I could be successful; I was already successful. After my arrest (but before serving my sentence), I focused on my construction business and started life over. So I did not get anything out of the chaplain's "you can do it" message.

After listening to my ranting and raving about the sermon, this inmate gave me something to think about. He wanted me to know that I was not supposed to go to the chapel to see what I could "get" from the service. I was to go there to worship God. I was to go there to give, not to take.

Going to church to worship and give was a new concept. I had gone to church my entire life to prove to God that I was a Christian. While I was married, I made sure our family went most Sundays. And going most Sundays made me feel responsible. Going most Sundays satisfied me that I had received enough from God to get me into heaven. I thought the only point of going to church was to get the message.

EXEMPLARY LIFE

As I continued to go to the chapel every week, there were other things that some of my inmate brothers pointed out to me. But one stands out above all others.

One day I was talking to Tim, the "do you want any food or anything" inmate. I had mentioned that I had been a Christian my entire life. I told him I went to a Lutheran school from kindergarten through eighth grade and attended church most weeks. Of course, I believed in Jesus.

Tim, not impressed with what I had done, asked me if I was saved. I was surprised he would ask that because of my Christian credentials. But I told him I was definitely saved and going to heaven. Then Tim asked me how I knew I was saved.

I gave him the standard Bible answer used by religious people worldwide. I told him that I knew I was saved because Jesus died for my sins. I think this was the same answer I gave back in first grade, an oldie but a goodie. I am not saying it is the wrong answer. But I would discover later that it is an incomplete answer.

Tim accepted this answer but pressed on with his "salvation knock-out punch." He asked me *when* I was saved.

What the heck did he mean by *when* did I get saved? I had no idea when I got saved. I just was. I told Tim I had always been saved because of the school, the church, my upbringing, blah, blah, blah. Tim listened to this, and we finished our conversation. He had performed his Christian duty. He made me realize that I was not 100 percent sure I was saved.

This conversation with Tim was a blessing. I cannot think of anything more important than knowing 100 percent where you are going after you die.

As a result, I began to study my Bible more and more. I started asking questions of Tim and other men I knew from the chapel. I scheduled a few appointments with the chaplains and attended

CHAPTER 42

Bible studies. I did my Bible correspondence courses as soon as they arrived, and I prayed often. But I also continued my other activities.

I continued to play softball, and I continued to play cards. I continued to read fiction mysteries and fantasy stories. But I did all those things less and focused more on my eternal future.

I remember when I got into a habit of playing cards almost daily. Tim noticed this and asked me a question that would change how I served my prison time. He asked me if, when I got home, I would ever look back on my time here and say, "Man, I wish I would have played more cards."

I loved that! I applied that thought to the rest of my time there in prison. I was not going to go home and say that I wish I had played more cards. Cards are merely a time passer like video games, golf, television, or many other things we devote ourselves to in our free time.

But what impact would it have on my being if I were to go home and think, *I wish I would have learned more about the Bible*? I understood the blessing of the time I had been given to read God's Word, and I was not going to waste any time. Bible study became a joy for me. It became something I would get to do instead of something I had to do.

We should all ask ourselves this question: Do you ever go to bed at night and think, *I wish I would have read my Bible today*? Do you think you will say that when you take the last breath of your life?

While you lie there, knowing that you are about to die, a thought might pop into your brain. *I wish I would have learned more about God's Word.* Do you think it might be a little late by then?

So when did I finally know that I was saved? When did I become a follower of Christ and not just one of His many fans?

I will cover that in the next chapter about forgiveness. It's about how the Lord helped me take words out of my mind and put them on paper.

Writing is not one of my favorite activities. I have always been more of a speaker, a presenter, a showman. But after I got saved, I began to take notes on everything I encountered that impacted me. They were simple one- or two-sentence things I picked up from the chapel services, my Bible studies, and correspondence courses, books, and conversations.

In late 2011, I went back through nearly two years of those notes that totaled over 50 pages of thoughts. I began praying to God about them. I felt there was a lot of stuff there that other people should know. But the idea of writing a book using an old prison typewriter was more than I was willing to take on.

In early 2012, there was an announcement that our prison library was getting new portable word processor machines. I would be able to check one out and work on this project. The word processor would allow me to spell check, copy and paste, and get my thoughts down in an organized manner.

So I began writing my first little project—the next chapter on forgiveness. It is the account of how I came to accept God's free gift of salvation and have 100 percent assurance of where I am going when I physically die.

Reflection Section for Chapters 34–42 available on page 223

CHAPTER 43

FORGIVENESS

Can you think of someone in your life who has wronged you? Was it a boss you bent over backward for, but he gave the promotion to someone else? Was it a best friend who stole the love of your life 15 years ago? Maybe it was a coach who ruined your child's desire to play a sport or an ex-spouse who, well, is an ex-spouse. What do you think of immediately after you think of that person? What do you think of the split second after that person's name and face pop into your head?

Do you say, "Well, they are out of my life now, so I don't let them affect me anymore"? Are you honest with yourself? Maybe you say, "I hate that person. I don't care if they are alive or dead as long as they are not around me. They are a complete waste of space, and I don't care about them." What do you think about them?

Early in my teaching career, I got called in as a substitute to teach high school biology for the remaining three quarters of the year. One of my teaching certificates is in high school general science but not specifically biology. I welcomed the challenge and did my best. I studied the material for hours every night and made sure I understood enough to explain it to the high school kids—even the super-smart ones.

I taught four sections of high school biology that year and received praise from the department head, the assistant principal, and even the principal.

At the end of the year, the principal (Big Jim) called me into his office. He said, "Scott, you did a great job. Would you be interested in teaching science here again next year?" I was thrilled. I had a job. There would be no looking for a position all summer, no interviews, no uncertainty. I could just relax that summer. I accepted the position, and Jim said he would call the regional office and get another waiver for me to be allowed to teach the class again. The waiver was necessary because I did not have the official biology certificate but the broader general science certificate.

Summer flew by as it does for most teachers. The assistant principal called me three weeks before school was scheduled to start. She was a very bubbly and helpful lady. I referred to her as Bubbles in my head. She asked me if I would consider teaching beginning chemistry instead of biology. I agreed. She told me to come in and pick up the teacher's manuals, which I did so I could start preparing.

The next three weeks went by quickly, and I spent most evenings preparing lesson plans. I would call and talk to the department head for advice on topics I did not quite understand.

Teaching high school science, biology, and chemistry was the most amazing turn of events. I barely graduated from high school, ranking number 301 out of 330 in my graduating class. It was a lack of effort more than a lack of ability. And here I was, about to teach high school chemistry. Only in America!

About three days before school started, my wife, also a teacher, got her schedule for when to report, but I did not.

I called my school and asked the secretary what day and time teacher meetings were held. She said they were at 8:00 a.m. in just two days. I could not wait.

CHAPTER 43

I showed up before 7:30 a.m. and was catching up on the summer with my colleagues when Bubbles approached me without showing her usual big, overdone smile. "Um, Scott, follow me. Jim [the principal] wants to talk to you." I followed her into the office and sat in the chair across from the secretary. It was about 7:45 a.m. I sat in that chair until just after 10:00 a.m. I felt like I was in junior high all over again.

Just before 10:00 a.m., I saw my colleagues scrambling around the halls, in and out of their classrooms, to the kitchen for coffee, lined up at the copy machines—just the common panicked movements of a group of teachers who just realized vacation was over. The strange thing, though, was that none of my colleagues were sitting in the office by the secretary.

Through the door came Big Jim. Then there went Big Jim, straight past me and into his office, door closed. This was not good. Even the assistant principal walked by me five or six times without a glance. I was beginning to think something was wrong. Actually, I had thought that for quite a while. I may have graduated number 301, but I wasn't the dullest tool in the shed.

At 10:35 a.m., Big Jim opened his door and walked out to his secretary. He handed her a sticky note and turned his head back to the confines of his den. With a curious look on his face, he glanced at me and said, "Are you waiting to see me?"

After answering with a humble yes, I walked into his office. Feeling something was wrong, I asked him, "What class am I teaching?"

Big Jim said, "Scott, I don't have a position for you. I called last week to get the waiver, and they won't give me one for the same person two years in a row. We are supposed to try to recruit someone to fill the position."

I just stood there for what seemed like forever but was more on the line of a few seconds. The most obvious question came into my head. I boldly said, "What am I supposed to do now?"

EXEMPLARY LIFE

Jim replied, "Are you on the substitute list?"

Seriously, why would I be signed up for the substitute list when I had been led to believe for the last three months that I had a full-time teaching job? He had not thought that far ahead before asking such an elementary question.

As I got up to leave Jim's office, he assured me they would call me to substitute "every day possible." I went straight to the district office, signed up to be a substitute again, and then headed home. I had to tell my wife that I did not have a job, a regular paycheck, free family insurance, or any other perks that went with being a respected high school chemistry teacher. I threw the teacher's manuals in the garbage. Two days later, my wife left for her teaching job, and I stayed home.

I developed a hatred for Jim when he said he did not have a teaching position for me. I considered him the one man who ruined my current life. I had done a great job teaching the year before. He had promised me security. And then he took it away with his carelessness. How could he wait until the week before school starts to check on my waiver? He then topped off his character by not even giving me a courtesy call to tell me.

How could he have Bubbles give me books to prepare with three short weeks before and then destroy my immediate future? She was just as guilty, always smiling and helpful but never looking at me while I waited in the office. I was no longer a colleague. She deserved my hate too.

During the first quarter of school, I got called almost every day to substitute somewhere in the district, but never once did I get called to fill in at Big Jim's school.

Three years later, Jim died of cancer. The district decided that the bubbly assistant principal was not a very good administrator and demoted her to being a regular teacher. I, however, was in my second year of full-time teaching and coaching and doing great.

CHAPTER 43

Because of Jim's carelessness toward me and my unwillingness to forgive his mistake, I carried a lot of hate for him and his assistant for over 15 years. I allowed Satan to control that part of my emotions for a long time. Thank God I did not die with that burden of unforgiveness.

I was reading my Bible sometime after my arrest when I came across a passage that caught my attention. In Matthew, Jesus was speaking to His disciples in what we know as the Sermon on the Mount. In Matthew 6:5–15 (NASB 1995), Jesus instructs us on how to pray. Verses 14 and 15 hit me like a ton of bricks.

Jesus said, "For if you forgive others for their transgressions, your heavenly Father will also forgive you. But if you do not forgive others, then your Father will not forgive your transgressions."

I read those two verses over and over. What exactly did Jesus mean that the "Father will not forgive your transgressions"? I began to ask myself that if God does not forgive me, how will I get to heaven?

From very early in my life, I knew I wanted to go to heaven when I died. There is a 100 percent chance that we will all die someday (unless we are alive when Christ returns). There is no 100 percent chance that we will all go to heaven.

A short time after I read this passage, I decided I needed to speak to my pastor, Wray, about my forgiveness issue. This was serious, and it was on my mind every day.

By the time I spoke with Wray, I had done a "forgiveness inventory" and realized that there were at least eight people in my past who I would never forgive. There were, of course, Jim and Bubbles, but there was also a high and mighty counselor, an overreacting athletic director, an unfair coach, a few lying detectives, and of course, a mother-in-law.

I told Pastor Wray that I was worried about God forgiving me. Wray asked me if I wanted to be able to forgive those people.

I replied that I undoubtedly wanted to forgive all the people in my life I had hated. I did not enjoy the feelings I had for these people. He told me that the first step in forgiveness was the desire to forgive, that forgiving is a process, and that forgiveness takes time.

That was not exactly what I wanted to hear. I am a get-it-done-now type of person. What I wanted was the secret forgiveness formula. I had hoped that Wray would be able to flip a switch in my brain that would allow me to forget the wrongs these people had done or, at the very least, be able to ignore what they had done to me—kind of a passive forgiveness was what I was shooting for.

I began to pray about forgiveness now and then, usually when something made me think about one of those people. It would start with a vision or an actual face-to-face encounter with one of the unforgiven.

Immediately I would think, "God, I forgive them." For some reason, that was not working. I said I forgave, but I did not feel the forgiveness. I was fooling myself into believing that if I could convince God I forgave them, He would forgive me. In my mind, forgiveness was cause and effect. That is not what forgiveness is. Forgiveness is not a thing we do. It is a thing we give. And to truly forgive, we must be willing to pray about it more than every now and then.

Several months passed, and I had made little progress in forgiving anyone on my hate list. I found that it was much easier just to ignore them. God, however, did not forget that I had a forgiveness issue.

While I was in prison, those Bible correspondence study courses were a great way to understand more of God's Word. After filtering through the many studies I had ordered and deciding which ones I liked and did not like, I ended up with six or seven that I studied regularly. I will never forget what I now call my Forgiveness Week.

CHAPTER 43

Sunday morning I went to the chapel for the regular Christian service. The sermon that day was on forgiveness, and the chaplain referred to Matthew 18:21–35. If you do not know this passage, please take a moment and read it now.

In summary, it is where Jesus tells Peter that you should forgive your enemies not up to seven times but up to seventy times seven times. Jesus then goes on to tell the story of the king who forgave the debt of a servant. But that servant went out and demanded payment from others who owed him. After hearing about this, the king was angry and handed the first servant over for torture until he could repay what was owed.

This is an excellent lesson on receiving and living out forgiveness. But the part that moved me the most was verse 35. At the end of the story, Jesus states, "My heavenly Father will also do the same to you, if each of you does not forgive his brother from your heart" (Matt. 18:35 NASB 1995).

This verse sounded much like the other passage from Matthew 6 I had read months before. When I returned to my cube, I searched for other forgiveness passages in my Bible. It took me well over an hour just to look them up and read them once. I went to bed that night, asking God if the chaplain was trying to tell me something.

Monday came around, and I had not opened my Bible yet. But I was still thinking about forgiveness and what the chaplain said. The mail call was at about 2:00 p.m., and one of my Bible correspondence courses showed up. I opened it and found in its pages a lesson about forgiveness.

I brushed this off as a coincidence—a powerful one for sure but not a God thing. It was just a random chance. But the timing was still pretty cool.

I did my study and put the answers in the mail. I prayed to God that night to help me forgive and thanked Him for the sign if He was responsible for it.

On Tuesday, another study came in the mail. I opened it immediately. Sure enough, the main topic was forgiveness. I looked at the addresses of the two studies to see if they were related. They had no connection to each other. You cannot imagine how that affected me.

I was convinced something was going on. God had my attention. For me, time was supposed to heal this problem. God had a different idea. God knew I had a slight desire to forgive, but I did not have the Holy Spirit residing in my heart. What I needed was a little push from Him.

I completed that Bible study and spent much of my time that day looking up passages on forgiveness. This time, though, I did more than just read the verses once. I wrote them down and checked cross references. For the first time in my life, I studied the Bible as I think God intended. That night, I prayed to God in a sincere, heartfelt way.

I was at the mail call early on Wednesday, but no Bible studies came. I did not expect it to happen a third time anyway, but I was there just in case. I had always believed that random chances happen once, maybe two times at the most. Besides, God was pretty convincing already.

On Thursday at the mail call, I did receive another one of my Bible correspondence studies, the third one that week. The thought was on my mind that there was no way this one had to do with forgiveness. I opened it in the hall on the way to my cube. And yes, it was on forgiveness.

After I opened it, I put it on my table and lay down on my bunk. I did not sleep. I did not pray. I talked to God. I had a real conversation with my Father. I confessed my deep-down feelings for all the people who were on my hate list. I reviewed each of the things they had done. And I asked God to take away my hate for them. I asked Him to come into my heart and fill it with the

CHAPTER 43

Holy Spirit so there was no room left for hate. I was not able to do that myself. I needed His help. At that moment, the Holy Spirit came into my body after 40-plus years of life.

While talking to God, I decided to say the Lord's Prayer to end my time with Him. I was very anxious to get to work on the new Bible study.

Have you ever recited the Lord's Prayer? Have you recited, not really prayed it, and said it? That was not what I was doing. I was sincerely praying the Lord's Prayer as God intended. And there, almost in the middle of it, was God's message to me about forgiveness again. I had never paid much attention to that part of the prayer.

Right after "Give us this day our daily bread" is "And forgive us our debts, as we also have forgiven our debtors" (Matt. 6:11–12 NASB 1995). I don't know about you, but I do not want God to forgive me in the same way I had been forgiving others.

If God forgave me like that, He would push me out of His mind. He would not think of me because when He did, He would experience all kinds of hate. Or He would forgive me by saying everything was okay because He doesn't care about me anymore. I would think I can live my life however I want because I can't affect Him as I did in the past. I wouldn't mean anything to Him now. He would be done with me.

These are not examples of forgiveness. I am glad God does not forgive me as I was (not) forgiving others.

God's help is needed for real, complete forgiveness. We are sinful beings. Our nature is to dislike those who have hurt us. Jeremiah 13:23 (NASB 1995) reads, "Can the Ethiopian change his skin or the leopard his spots? Then you also can do good who are accustomed to doing evil." This analogy tells us that we cannot change our sinful natures by ourselves. Only God can change a sinner's heart.

God came into my life the moment I asked Him to during my Forgiveness Week. The Holy Spirit came into my heart, and I accepted Christ as the guide to my life. I became a new creature in Christ. He is my Lord and Savior.

I've heard the question, "How fully does God actually forgive us?" You can find the answer in Isaiah 43:25 (NASB 1995). God states, "I, even I, am the one who wipes out your transgressions for My own sake, and I will not remember your sins." And He forgives so completely because God's son, Jesus, died on the cross to pay for our sins, and He rose again, conquering sin and death.

Just imagine that. All the things you have done wrong in your life will be forgiven and forgotten by God if you accept Jesus's gift of salvation. God loves us so much that He gave his Son to die in our place so we can spend eternity with Him. How incredible!

By believing in your heart and confessing with your mouth that Jesus is your Lord and Savior, by asking Him to forgive your sins and by forgiving others, you will receive this incredible gift.

Ephesians 4:31-32 (NASB 1995) tells us to "let all bitterness and wrath and anger and clamor and slander be put away from you, along with all malice. Be kind to one another, tender-hearted, forgiving each other, just as God in Christ also has forgiven you."

We find a similar passage in Colossians 3:12-13 (NASB 1995). "So, as those who have been chosen of God, holy and beloved, put on a heart of compassion, kindness, humility, gentleness, and patience; bearing with one another, and forgiving each other, whoever has a complaint against anyone; just as the Lord forgave you, so also should you."

It is clear that God expects us to forgive each other's transgressions. It is also clear that God expects us to forgive others entirely. Forgiving others is something God instructs us to put in our prayers.

CHAPTER 43

Mark 11:25 (NASB 1995) states, "Whenever you stand praying, forgive, if you have anything against anyone, so that your Father who is in heaven will also forgive you your transgressions."

I was guilty of not putting forgiveness in my prayers. When I did start including forgiveness in my prayers, it was in a secondary role. My prayers usually began by trying to butter God up by telling Him how awesome He is. Then I went into everything I wanted (the longest part of the prayer). I would explain to God different ideas of how He could help me get those things, which included a timeline to get those things. And finally, I would ask God to forgive my sins.

For me, unforgiveness was a major issue. But it took a minor role in my prayers. Eventually, I gave forgiveness a significant, headline role in my prayers.

Jesus ties forgiveness to all kinds of praying. He says to forgive whenever we pray. It does not matter what you are praying for or about. Take care of your forgiveness issues first. Successful prayer requires forgiveness as well as faith.

God puts so much emphasis on forgiving others in our prayers that I wonder how much our prayers mean to Him if we refuse to address our forgiveness issues. Without forgiveness, are we praying to God or are we praying so we will feel better? "Alrighty, God, I prayed today. Check."

If you do not have forgiveness for someone who has harmed you, do you think it is pretty prideful to ask God to forgive you?

I thought I was number one, that I could steer my life on my own and architect my circumstances in the best manner for me. Sure, I cared about others, but when it came down to the core of my beliefs, I was number one, and surely God should forgive me no matter how I felt about others. That is a prideful mindset. God is not a big fan of prideful people. (See Proverbs 16:18 and 1 John 2:16 for examples.)

If you refuse to forgive someone in your life, then it is time to ask for God's help. No matter how much people have wronged you, you have wronged God greatly in your life. In other words, the chasm between you and the person who wronged you is much smaller than the chasm between you and the Holy God who offers you forgiveness via Jesus.

Do you say you love God? Do you have hate in your heart for anyone? You cannot answer yes to both of these questions.

Many of the men I got to know in prison spoke to me about someone they hated, someone they said they will never forgive. Some of these men claimed to be Christians. Based on their unwillingness to forgive, I have to question their interpretation of being saved.

One striking passage in the Bible on this topic is 1 John 4:19–20 (NASB 1995), which reads, "We love, because He first loved us. If someone says, 'I love God,' and hates his brother, he is a liar; for the one who does not love his brother whom he has seen, cannot love God whom he has not seen."

Again the message is sent. You cannot have hate for others and still love God. You can claim to love God, but God is not to be fooled.

Some of the men I have talked to have used the excuse that they are not forgiving these hated people in their lives because they don't deserve forgiveness.

I ask, what do you think that person is getting from your forgiving them? They benefit very little compared to what you get from giving forgiveness.

By forgiving someone else, you are getting the approval of God. You are getting a God who will listen to your prayers. You are on your way to eternal life. The other person is receiving your forgiveness. You are not giving them a gift. You are giving yourself a gift.

CHAPTER 43

There might be a residual effect to your forgiveness, though. The forgiven just might see you acting like a follower of Christ. And they may decide someday, due to the seed you planted, to follow Christ also.

Hatred for others separates us from God. In 1 John 2:9-11 (NASB 1995), God's Word says, "The one who says he is in the Light and *yet* hates his brother is in the darkness until now. The one who loves his brother abides in the Light and there is no cause for stumbling in him. But the one who hates his brother is in darkness and walks in the darkness, and does not know where he is going because the darkness has blinded his eyes."

When you hate, you are blind to God. Forgiving another person is a washing away of that darkness. It allows the Light, God, to work in your life. No darkness abides in God. You cannot have it both ways. You cannot hate another person and still love God.

It is possible to forgive someone no matter how they have wronged you. Look at Jesus as an example. He was wrongly convicted. He was tortured, abandoned, and humiliated. He was executed in an excruciating manner. And yet while he was hanging on the cross, he said, "Father forgive them; for they do not know what they are doing" (Luke 23:34 NASB 1995). That is the ultimate forgiveness.

Do not let Satan have power over you and convince you that you cannot forgive someone because their transgression is worse than all your sins against God. Let Jesus be your example. Ask God for His help, and let the Light shine in your life. It is an eternal decision.

Reflection Section for Chapter 43 available on page 226

CHAPTER 44

Forty-three chapters ago, you began reading this book. I hope my story has helped you in some way.

This is not a fictional or embellished book. This entire story, every part of it, and every character on these pages are true. Nothing has been made up or added for effect.

I want to tell you that if you are doing something you should not be doing, you should stop today. It does not matter who condones your behavior, even if it is your family. It does not matter if no one knows about your behavior. You know, and you need to ask yourself, "What if someone finds out?"

My story is not about what can happen if you acquire illegal online videos. That is just my experience, the specifics of my general brokenness.

What about you? Do you regularly skim money out of the cash drawer at work because the guy before you skimmed money? Let me guess. It's only a few dollars compared to what is in there. The company will never miss it.

Do you only buy drugs now and then for "personal recreation?" After all, isn't it your right to put whatever you want into your body?

CHAPTER 44

Do you drink too much and then drive? Have you? Ever? I did in my younger days. And I am lucky that in all the times I did, I never had an accident that killed someone.

These are just three examples of things that can put you in lockup. They are just three activities that, if discovered, will likely take you away from your family. They are just three negative examples waiting to be discovered by your children.

Are you ignoring things in your life that are just a "little illegal?" I did. I knew for a fact the first time an illegal child video came on my computer that it was something I should avoid. But I kept downloading because I justified in my mind that since it was not what I was looking for, and I was deleting them as soon as I saw what they were, my actions were okay.

Two weeks before my arrest, the local news reported that six men were arrested for the same kinds of videos that were coming onto my computer. And I still ignored it, believing that I was different. I would never get arrested because my intentions were not the same as theirs.

How many times have you heard news about a drunk driver killing someone? You drink and then drive, but you are a much more careful drunk driver, right?

How often have you read about someone getting shot in a drug deal? But you don't buy from those types of people, right?

How frequently have you heard of an executive skimming a little extra spending money from the company books? But you only take a few bucks.

I won't go on any more about this. I hope none of these examples apply to you. If you are a non-believer in Christ, you have nothing stopping you except your moral convictions. I hope that is enough. If you find yourself in a jail cell, your morals will not help or even comfort you.

One last thing for any non-Christians as this book is about to end. I have added—for the benefit of my fellow Christians—a short message at the back of the book. I have received salvation through Christ Jesus, and I want to tell others about it. I hope you decide to read on.

I will finish by writing that if you don't get anything else from this book, I hope you get this: Please, don't do careless things that could put you in prison and take you away from your family.

A MESSAGE TO MY FELLOW CHRISTIANS

I am humbled that you have made it to this page in my book. You are giving me a great gift. My hope for this entire project has been to help others spiritually. I would like to believe that if you have continued to read this far, you are gaining something from it.

I have attempted to help the non-believers subliminally. On the surface, I want them to stay out of trouble, be good people, and care for their families. But I have a greater desire for them.

In this story, I have mentioned God enough that a seed has been planted. I desire that sometime in the future, at least one of the non-believing readers will turn to Christ because of my testimony.

My message to the rest of you will not be subliminal. God's Word is truly alive. It is not old and dead and for us to refer back to only when times are tough. God's messages to us are coming every day. We need to search for them, find them, and apply them. As a Christian, are you doing these things?

It was not until I accepted salvation that I deeply desired to study God's Word. Whenever I came across something that was speaking to me, I wrote it down. I encourage you to do the same. It will draw you into a closer relationship with God.

I am not under a delusion that I am a Bible scholar. I am not. At 48 years old, I am a baby Christian, but I am maturing every day. I am a man who has had some experiences I hope will help others avoid. But I am also a man who, because of those experiences, now has the Holy Spirit living in me.

I want to take a moment to clean up a topic that I started at the beginning of this book. I referred to my "three lives." Let me explain.

I consider my first life the time before I got arrested—from when I was born until right before those seven police cars drove down my street and surrounded my house. I was blessed with a wonderful wife and two great sons in my first life. I had a rewarding teaching and coaching career and all the respect on a human level that I ever wanted. Money was not a problem. Some might have looked at my life and thought I was living the American dream. And to top off my first life, I thought I had an insurance policy with God.

I thought I gave my premiums every week or two by attending church. I assumed I paid my "God premiums" by praying with my sons every night. I tried to pay these premiums by being a "good guy." But the fact is, I was in charge of my life, not God.

My second life was a transition period in my existence. I changed into a man who is still sinful but trying to let God direct his path. I entered prison, a man bound for hell. I left prison, a man being led by God on the path to eternal salvation.

God has used this experience to work in my heart, soul, and mind. And I have used my free will to allow Him to do that. Accepting salvation is a choice that God gives each of us.

I wake up every day a different being than I used to be. One of my favorite Bible passages is 2 Corinthians 5:17 (NASB 1995), which says, "Therefore if anyone is in Christ, *he is* a new creature; the old things passed away; behold, new things have come."

Notice that this passage does not say I am a new man. It says I am a new creature. I love that! I know now that Christ is in me; I am not the same thing I used to be. Not only that, but I cannot return to being that old hell-bound thing. I am a new creature. The old thing has passed away.

And that brings me to the most exciting time of all. I had never experienced the free world as the new creature I am. I had only experienced prison as a man with salvation. My third life began when I walked out of the prison doors on May 7, 2013, at 7:00 a.m. Seeing how God has been using me in my third life has been incredible!

Finally, I hope this book will be a tool for you to spread the Word of God to others. You probably know someone—maybe a neighbor or someone you work with—who has not accepted the Lord as their Savior. Please lend them a copy of this book if you think it can help send the message. I hope reading these pages will cause others to evaluate their lives. Maybe this will plant the seed of salvation in them so they might also find Christ someday. I would be honored if you would help me spread the Word and do His work.

EPILOGUE

So here I am, 10 years into my third life. I am writing this final piece to update a story that seems to have just happened but also seems so long ago. Life in the "free world" as a felon has not always been easy. But I assure you, as you read, it does get better—much better. God is good.

After my 1,115 days in federal prison, I spent five months in a halfway house to reintegrate into society. I got a job painting houses and was able to reconnect with old friends. I found a friendly church close to the halfway house. After receiving approval, I went every Sunday.

After leaving the halfway house, I moved to Florida where my ex-wife, her new husband, and my sons had relocated. My brother and his wife lived in the same town and allowed me to move in with him for a few months while I looked for a permanent place to live.

I had to serve five years on probation, which was challenging at times. As part of the conditions of my release on probation, I was required to attend counseling every week with a group of nine other guys who were registered sex offenders. I often shared with that group how God had worked in my life. Dr. Bill, who led the group, told me numerous times, "God was not a part of

EPILOGUE

the treatment." He repeatedly reminded the group that God was often an excuse that offenders used to make it seem like they were doing fine when they were not. They were hiding behind God or whatever higher power they wanted so they could continue their old actions and old thoughts.

His words often made me angry. I had found such joy, peace, and growth in Christ that I knew it was real. I endured the program but found little support from it for my walk with Christ. As a newer Christian, I realized Satan was upping his attack using authority figures.

My probation officer, Anna, was known to be the toughest probation officer. She was the Senior Probation Officer and claimed to be in control of the worst offenders. In our first meeting, she warned me that I "may have fooled the federal judge and prosecutor, but I was not fooling her." She was sure I was sick, and it was "just a matter of time before she hauled me back in front of the judge for a violation," and I would go back to prison.

Anna needed to know what church I would attend and met with the associate pastor, Jason. I had already met with him and shared my whole story, but Anna's story must have been quite an exaggeration. Jason asked to meet with me again and bring the court transcripts to prove what I had told him was true. He told me Anna wanted me to check in with the security staff when I arrived, have them escort me to my seat, and not sit within three seats of anyone else. And if I had to use the restroom, I was to be escorted by security.

After Jason read the court transcripts, he told me he did not feel any of Anna's requirements were necessary. Then he did something I should have thought of. He suggested we pray for Anna. We did, right there in his office.

I continued to pray for Anna now and then, usually when she upset me, which was often. God must have heard my prayers. After about 16 months, Anna released me from her control and handed me over to a junior probation officer. He and my third probation officer were much more accepting of my walk with Christ. It was great to be out of prison, but life was very challenging, especially as a new Christian.

Over time I gained a better understanding of the demanding, high-pressure job of being a probation officer. They had to keep track of 50 to 70 probationers at a time. If any of those people broke probation, the probation officer was accountable.

Acceptance into society was not what I expected. In my first life, I had a college degree. I had built houses. I had coached. I was educated, responsible, and hard-working. Who wouldn't want to hire me? Well, I soon learned almost nobody would hire me now.

Being on the sex offender list made getting hired for any job nearly impossible. The sex offender list includes everyone from those convicted of child molestation to those who had inadvertently allowed child pornography to come on their computer. The actual crime did not matter.

One of the first jobs I had, technically speaking, was at a local chain grocery store. I filled out the application in person and checked the little box on the back that said I had a felony. I wrote "possession of child pornography" on the line. I handed the application to the manager. She interviewed me for about 10 minutes for a deli position and then offered me the job. I was thrilled!

We talked a little more about the duties, and then she walked into the back room to get some hiring paperwork. When she returned, she said she was sorry but they cannot hire sex offenders. A corporate memo had been issued stating no offenders would be hired, and all currently employed offenders must be let go.

I was confused and upset. I would have been behind the deli counter making sandwiches, cleaning, and doing deli things. I

EPILOGUE

asked why she couldn't hire me for this position, and she said it must have been a liability issue.

I proceeded to get turned down for every other job there was. It almost made me laugh when I was turned down to operate a draw bridge. For this job, I would sit inside a tiny booth by myself for eight hours a day and raise the draw bridge if a boat approached. There would be no contact with anyone, but they could not hire me because I am a sex offender.

Another interview was with a small painting and remodeling company. The owner and I talked at length. He was impressed by my construction experience and offered me the job. I mentioned that he didn't ask about my criminal history. His exact reply was, "As long as you're not a sex offender, its fine." I used my quick wit, looked him in the eye, and said, "Nope, I killed two people with a circular saw." After a few moments of awkward silence, I said to him, yes, I have a sex offense. He did not care what it was, but he could not hire me. He said, "I have a wife to answer to, and she would never allow it."

Over the next six weeks, I spent eight hours a day looking for a job and had nothing to show for my efforts. Most of the time, when I clicked the box admitting to having a felony, a message would come up stating they do not hire felons at this time. The interviews I got all went well until my criminal record came up. Being on the sex offender list or having a felony was always a deal breaker. I realized the seriousness of my situation and prayed throughout the day that God would let me get a job. I prayed before every interview, but nothing panned out.

I had some savings from before I went to prison and lived off that. But with moving expenses, rent, car payment, food, and other necessities, my resources were dwindling quickly. I decided that when my savings hit two months of funds, I would cash out my teacher's retirement plan. Cashing out early would penalize me about 40 percent, but what choice did I have? I needed to live. I had been told that a vast number of sex offenders are homeless. Without jobs, they cannot find a place to live. I did not want to be in that group, but I was headed that way.

I had served my time. I had given my life to the Lord and was trying my best to honor Him. Why was God not coming through with a job?

I had a date on my calendar to call the teacher's retirement system and request the early withdrawal of all my retirement money, and it was fast approaching. It was a poor financial decision, but I was desperate. The date arrived, and I still had no job, so I made the call. I was reminded of the significant penalties, but I went through with it. I was at my financial lowest.

Three days after cashing out my retirement, I noticed a recycling center and decided to see if they were hiring. I walked in to inquire, and the secretary asked, "Can you talk to customers?" I replied that I had taught school, coached, and had no problem talking to anyone. She asked if I could wait 20 minutes. She gave me an application and said, "William will want to talk to you. We lost our delivery driver yesterday."

Yesterday? And here I randomly walked in today. I had applied for so many jobs. Why had I not seen this place weeks ago? Oh, wait. They were not hiring then. As I filled out the application, I noticed it did not say "recycling" but instead "portables." I asked her what that was. She said the recycling center was the next trailer over; this was the office for the portable toilets. I shrugged and said, "Okay." I needed a job. I did not care what I was delivering.

William interviewed me, and after we talked for a while, I told him I was on the sex offender list. To my surprise, he did not care. He had a few other employees who were on the list. I did all I could not to jump up and hug him right then.

EPILOGUE

William hired me at $2 an hour above minimum wage. He did not care how much I worked, and I could collect whatever overtime I needed to complete the job. During my first 14 weeks there, I worked over 75 hours each week. The overtime was like an extra paycheck.

I worked as a delivery driver for about four months before I was promoted to yard manager. I worked in that position for almost a year before I was promoted to work in the office. My responsibilities grew, and with God's help, I increased the business fourfold.

I worked there for over seven years, made decisions contributing to almost every part of the company's growth, and gained a wealth of knowledge about running a business. One of the most rewarding parts of that job was that I also was involved in hiring. I contacted the local halfway house and hired multiple drivers and yard workers who were criminals, including sex offenders. Most of those people were so grateful to have jobs that they were some of our best employees. They just needed a second chance.

I was getting a raise every six months, and within about four years, I was making more than I had made as a teacher and a coach. This financial blessing allowed me to purchase a house—no more renting. I now had a home of my own.

I have often looked back on the disappointing job interviews, and I did not understand why God took so long to answer my prayers. But if He had let me become a draw bridge operator, I would have missed a much better opportunity in the portable toilet industry. (It's okay to laugh. This entire process has taught me a lot about humility!)

This job was a blessing for seven years. Then God provided a chance for me to buy a turnkey operation in part of the hobby industry I had been in and out of since I was a kid. I have been the owner of this company now for three years. I am blessed every day to commute through the kitchen to my home office and do something I love.

I was not always patient when I was looking for that first job after prison, and I didn't understand why it was such a struggle. But I did always trust that God would provide. I just needed to stay faithful and remember He was in control and had a plan for me. It was not easy, but God has provided.

Besides employment, another area of unacceptance was the church. Well, I was accepted, and then I wasn't, which cut me to the core. I had been attending a church with the most incredible worship that was genuinely next level, but the sermons were pretty basic. In my four years there, I went from attending to serving on the greeter team and then accepted the assistant leader role on the team. I was asked to join a new training program for church leadership. I was also asked to lead a small group at my house, which I did for two semesters.

But then it all ended. One Sunday when I was greeting, Jenna, one of the church staff, asked me if I could meet with her and Pastor Josh on Wednesday. I asked her what the topic was. She said they had a new sex offender policy.

I showed up at Josh's office, and he and Jenna looked uncomfortable. Josh said we would open with prayer, and he wanted me to know they loved me and had been forced to make some changes. He then started to tell me that he didn't want me to be angry. I interrupted and suggested that he open with prayer before going further. He prayed.

Josh slid the new sex offender policy across the table to me. He told me that if I wanted to continue attending church there, I would need to sign it and abide by it. With the new rules, I could no longer lead or serve on any team or lead a small group. If I wanted to attend a small group, the leadership would have to pick

EPILOGUE

which group, meet with the leader to explain my history as a sex offender, and see if they would accept me. Further, to continue going to church, I would need to call in advance and let them know which service I would attend, report straight to security when I got there, and be escorted to a seat. I could not use the restroom without a security escort and would need to leave right after the service. I must go directly to my car—no talking with friends in the lobby.

As you can imagine, I was quite upset. I asked Josh why this was happening, and he said it was "suggested by the church's lawyers for liability reasons." He asked, "How would it look if you were shaking hands at the door, and someone recognized you as a sex offender? All the kids come in those doors with their parents." I looked at him and said, "It would look like forgiveness—redemption."

Josh gave no response. I asked him why now? He knew the whole story and had read through all the court transcripts. He knew me after four years of attending and serving. Josh replied, "Well, I know *your* side of the story.» I was livid. I told him I would not sign it and would find a new church. The feeling of rejection was excruciating, especially from your church family.

But I had been praying about staying at that church for almost a year. Although I loved the worship and formed meaningful friendships, the sermons were superficial. I needed more meat. I had been praying to God but not taking action.

Two weeks before this meeting with Josh and Jenna, I had met Michelle. She had only attended my church a few times in the past and had her own church. She didn't enjoy the rock concert-type worship and found the messages too shallow. "It might be okay for a new believer," she said, "but I don't think it's a good place to stay if you want to grow." She was thrilled when I asked if I could start going to church with her.

EXEMPLARY LIFE

I started attending Michelle's church the following Sunday. After I was there about a year, the lead pastor, Joe, asked if I could come in for a meeting. He said someone had notified them that I was on the sex offender list, and he would like me to come in and meet with them. Here we go again.

Michelle knew what happened at my previous church and was unhappy that it might happen again. She had been at this church for 15 years. She knew almost everyone and wondered who had the time to look me up and report me to the pastor. Why would they not just come to her?

Michelle said I was not going to this meeting alone. Pastor Joe, Pastor Joel, and an elder were there when we walked in. There was one extra open seat for me. They got a chair for Michelle.

Joe started by telling me how much they loved me, and he wanted to go through the policy with me and see how they could continue serving me as a church. The policy had three levels. One was for violent sex offenders, almost identical to the policy my old church wanted me to sign. The second was for child offenders. It included not entering the children's areas and requiring a chaperone to use the bathroom. The third was for general sex offenders, the least intrusive. Joe explained that they wanted to put me in the middle level. When he was done speaking, I asked him if he knew any details about my crime. He did not.

The three church leaders were very attentive as they listened to me share the whole story. After I finished, Pastor Joe asked if I could bring my book manuscript in so he could read it. He also wanted to see the court documents that backed up what I told him. I agreed to bring them back later that day.

A few days later, Joe emailed me and asked if Michelle and I could come back in and have another meeting. Joe had researched everything and prayed about it. He thought that at the most I should be on the lowest level, which primarily meant avoiding the kids' area. With great sincerity, he also said how much they loved Michelle and me.

It has been a few years since that meeting, and we have never felt slighted. The church has been such a great blessing to us. Summit Church at Gateway in Fort Myers, Florida, truly lives out the all-inclusive love of Jesus. We enjoy serving on the host team and participating in small groups and men's and women's ministries. As true representatives of Christ, our church accepts, loves, and includes us. God has welcomed me into this family through these pastors, and I am truly grateful.

Besides rejection from employers and a church, there have been others who have turned their backs on me since my release from prison. Most people were in shock or disbelief when I shared my story, but they were also gracious and supportive. However, a few people were totally closed off and unwilling to hear any details. They only knew that I was on the sex offender list, and their minds were made up. There seems to be a commonality among people with this reaction. They or a close family member have gone through some sort of sexual abuse, and they have not experienced healing or forgiveness.

This always saddens me deeply. When these people hear just the topic of my crime, they have painful memories that still haunt them decades later. That is the work of Satan. Whenever that happens, I pray they will be able to release their hurt and find healing, that they will discover the peace, forgiveness, and love of Jesus as I have, whether they ever listen to my story or not.

Since I left prison, the relationships with my sons have been another challenge. When I was arrested, they were 10 and seven. When I left for prison, they were 12 and nine. When I next saw them, they were 16 and 13. I missed so much of their young lives. I called them on the phone every day of the 1,115 days I was in prison, but they didn't always answer. My younger son once told me that sometimes when we talked, it made him sad because he wanted me to come home. That devastated me, but I still called every night, hoping they would answer.

There were some concerns when I first got down to Florida and was reconnecting with my sons. My older son told me if this book were published and people found out about me, it might reflect negatively on his mom, a teacher in the school system there. The way he said it seemed strange to me. But my sons were still in school, and I did not want to make it hard on them, so I decided to delay publishing this book.

They are now 23 and 26 and have come through such a difficult situation in a way I cannot help but be proud of. My younger son got his firefighting and EMT certificates and joined the Marines. He is currently stationed in Japan, and we hear from him every few months. My older son graduated from college and works on the other side of the state managing a team at a time-share management company. We talk just about every week.

There has been a significant change from those little guys who would not let me go when I left for prison to the independent young men they are today. They do not attend church, but they have a foundation. They both know how important Michelle's and my relationship with the Lord is, and we pray for them daily. It would mean so much to me if everyone reading this book said a quick prayer for them to open their hearts to Christ. It took me 43 years to open mine. I hope it takes them less time.

My third life has had plenty of challenges, but each roadblock and hurdle has made me stronger and more confident that God is leading my life. I am aware of and grateful for so many blessings. Early in this book I mentioned that I grew up without a father. My dad divorced my mother when I was five. I had visitations with him on and off until I was 13, and then he left Illinois and moved to Florida. I talked to my dad two times in the next 35 years. When I moved to Florida, I found that my dad lived in the town next to where my ex-wife, sons, and brother live. I decided to reach out to him.

He was excited to hear from me, and we went to lunch. We have now been going to lunch every two or three weeks for the last 10 years. If it were not for the love of Jesus coming into my life and teaching me about forgiveness, I am not sure if I ever would have reached out to my dad. I have never felt hate for him. He just did not exist. But he has expressed many times how much he regretted not being there for me. I have told him each time that it is fine. What is important is that we are getting this time together. He is 86 now and still in good health. I have been blessed to have a great time getting to know him because I did not let Satan convince me that I needed to hold a grudge.

Another great blessing since being released from prison was meeting my wife, Michelle. I had decided to not date until after my boys were out of high school. After they graduated, I set up a profile on a dating app and started swiping through all the women who were supposedly my "perfect match."

After several failed dates, I came across Michelle's profile. She was beautiful, and I clicked on her information, which began with this: "I am a Christian woman. If you are not a Christian man, I am not interested." So I sent her a message.

I told her I was a Christian man, and we messaged back and forth for a few days before talking on the phone. Our conversations went so well that we agreed to meet for a drink. My first thought when I saw her was, "Wow! She's out of my league." She later admitted that she initially thought I had lied about my age due to my silver hair that had completely turned before I was 35. After some initial nerves, we hit it off.

We continued seeing each other, and I soon realized what a remarkable, godly woman she was. After a few weeks, I decided to tell her about my background. I did not want to let this relationship build any further without her knowing. I sat her down on her couch and told her I had a DVD for her to watch.

Do you remember that video I recorded before I left for prison—the one that was played for the congregation at my church? I played that video for Michelle and held my breath as she took in the information. When it was over, she had tears in her eyes. I told her she could ask me anything, and we talked for a few hours. She was understanding and gracious.

I had always hoped God would bring me someone special to spend my life with. God went above and beyond with Michelle. She is as beautiful on the inside as she is on the outside. She is a prayer warrior and a wonderful mother to her two sons who are now out of high school.

We met in December 2018, got engaged in December 2019, and married on Christmas Eve of 2020—over Zoom during the COVID pandemic with my pastor, Wray, from Illinois officiating. Michelle and I both had significant and difficult life experiences before God brought us together. We know God had a purpose for us and was preparing us for each other.

In closing, I'll share a few lessons learned from my battle with Satan and his destructive temptations. Satan will give you what you think you want. If you open the door to secret, sinful behaviors, no matter what they are, Satan will fuel them. Looking at pornography, having lunch with that woman at the office, gambling here and there, fudging the numbers a little at work—it seems so easy, even harmless. But it's anything but. Actions that don't honor God and habits we wouldn't be comfortable with everyone knowing will only lead to pain. It is essential to be on guard daily, and we can only do that through an honest relationship with Christ, by reading God's Word, and by being accountable to another mature Christian.

EPILOGUE

Repentance and forgiveness are long, difficult processes. When sinful habits are engrained in your life for a long time as mine were, they can take equally long to overcome. If you honestly inventory your life and spot any sinful habits, you can reach out to God for help now and avoid letting Satan get a bigger foothold.

God is faithful. When my first life fell apart, I would have never been able to see that God would restore me to the blessed life I enjoy today. Even though I chose to step into sin and away from God's plan for me, He was faithful to forgive me and accept me when I turned to Him. No matter what sins you may find yourself in, God wants to forgive you and restore you. You just need to ask.

My purpose in writing this book was for God to open doors for others who deal with sinful habits, hang-ups, and failures—and help them avoid the incredible loss I had to experience. I hope my story can bring insight and courage to others who are struggling with Satan's attacks. Living through all these things has never made me question the power of God, but it has made me aware that I cannot succeed without Him. I need Him every day, not just when I make terrible mistakes.

I am still a work in progress, but I now have a much stronger personal faith, the incredible peace of giving and receiving forgiveness, joy from the certainty of my salvation, overwhelming gratitude, and awe of God's incredible grace. Thank you for reading my story. I hope you can experience God's love, grace, and mercy as I have in this third life.

REFLECTION SECTION

Section 1: Chapters 1–7
DEVASTATION / SHOCK

Section 2: Chapters 8–17
SEPARATION FROM LOVED ONES

Section 3: Chapters 18–24
FACING HARD FACTS

Section 4: Chapters 25–33
SENTENCE HANDED DOWN

Section 5: Chapters 34–42
DESTINATION

Section 6: Chapter 43
FORGIVENESS

REFLECTION SECTION

Section 1: Chapters 1–7
DEVASTATION / SHOCK

1. Are there things you have done in your life that would devastate you if they were known publicly? Why do we want to keep our sins hidden and private?

   Read 2 Samuel 11:27–12:13.
   King David, like Scott, did not view his lust as any big deal. Life went on. For David it was a visit from the Prophet Nathan that brought the horrible truth to light. For Scott, it was a visit from law enforcement.

   Thought:
   Sin thrives under the cover of darkness and secrecy. In addiction recovery, we call this "living in denial." No recovery or growth can happen until we face the reality of our own sinfulness.

   Read John 16:7–8.
   Who helps bring us under conviction?

   Read Psalm 139:23–24.
   How can this openness to God help keep us from hiding sin in our hearts?

2. Why do you think God brought it down on Scott so hard?

Thought:
Almost in a heartbeat, Scott lost nearly everything he held dear, especially the trust and respect of his hometown, his fellow educators, his church, and his family.

Read James 1:2–4.
What loss have you experienced that God later turned to blessing?

Read Hebrews 12:7–11.
When does peace and righteousness finally come?

Pray Psalm 139:23–24 together.

REFLECTION SECTION

Section 2: Chapters 8–17
SEPARATION FROM LOVED ONES

1. Have you ever been separated from your immediate family for a period of time? Even forcibly? Even when they were close by? How did you handle it?

   Read 2 Timothy 4:16–17.
   Where did Paul find his comfort and strength? Did you ever experience this when Jesus was all you had?

   Thought:
   Scott loved being a dad to his two sons, especially since he was raised without a father. To be denied access to his sons was one of the hardest blows at this point in his story. He prayed hard about this, but he didn't just pray—he fought fiercely for the right to see his children. A mature Christian friend once said, "We should pray as if everything depended on God. We should work as if everything depended on us."

   Do you agree or disagree? How have you seen this truth play out in your own life?

2. Hope was in short supply at this point in Scott's journey. Have you ever found yourself at a place where everything seemed hopeless?

EXEMPLARY LIFE

Read Romans 15:4.
Where does this Scripture encourage us to go in such times?

Read Romans 5:3–5.
According to this passage, is hope immediately given or a process over time?
How have you experienced this?

Thought:
There were people God put in Scott's life who brought him hope and encouragement, people such as Loren and Jeanie who showed compassion and understanding.

Have you experienced God sending people into your life unexpectedly to bring hope?

Read Hebrews 13:5–6.
How might these words sustain you when everything seems to be going in the wrong direction?

Read Matthew 28:20, and thank Jesus for this promise.

REFLECTION SECTION

Section 3: Chapters 18–24
FACING HARD FACTS

1. Have you ever been at a place in life where things looked bleak and uncertain, but suddenly the situation took a turn for the worse? What did you do? Where did you turn to survive?

   Thought:
   In the local county court, Scott worked with a friend who was a lawyer. Suddenly Scott was informed that his case had been referred to federal court where the game is played differently. In 98 percent of cases that go to federal court, the defendant is found guilty. Mandatory sentences are imposed many times, and almost always it means time in prison. Scott realized he needed counsel who was familiar with federal court and sought a new lawyer. Things looked bleak!

   Read Luke 12:11–12.
   What is the source of the right words to defend yourself?

   Have you ever been in a situation where you had to rely on the Holy Spirit to give you the very words you were to say?

   Share your experience.

2. What would you share with a friend who comes to understand

that doing time in prison is on the horizon?

Read Philippians 4:12–13.
What comfort might this Scripture be? Where was Paul when he wrote these words?

Read 2 Corinthians 12:9.
How might this promise from God be reassuring? Have you ever stood on this promise?

Thought:
Having at least one person who believes in you is crucial in life. Scott's new lawyer, Steve Beckett, was a godsend. After they met with Detective Welker, Scott asked Beckett directly, "Do you believe I'm telling the truth, and do you accept my story as right?" His lawyer gave him a resounding vote of confidence, stating that he would never have taken his case if he didn't believe in him. That was huge for Scott.

Read 1 John 2:1–2 and Romans 8:34.
What comfort does it give you to know you have a great defense attorney in heaven?

Do you have confidence that Jesus believes in you?

Do you ever thank Jesus for defending you?

REFLECTION SECTION

3. Have you had to deal with your own pride when others were accusing you? Often we can't hear the truth another person might speak because we're too proud to admit our own faults.

Thought:
One of the hardest things Scott had to face was when a neighbor yelled at him about his attitude and that he thought he was better than everybody else. Although that made Scott very angry at the time, it caused him to reflect on his attitude. Pride can be a very subtle thing, which God would later help Scott face.

Read Romans 12:3 and Philippians 2:3.
Are you able to live this truth? Have you ever felt that sharing failures would make you weaker, never realizing it would really make you stronger?

Close by reading 1 Peter 5:5, and ask God to keep you humble at all times.

EXEMPLARY LIFE

Section 4: Chapters 25–33
SENTENCE HANDED DOWN

Most of us have faced consequences for our actions at some level, whether it was paying a traffic fine, making a late payment on a credit card that cost us dearly, or getting a bad grade in school because we neglected to study. But facing consequences for a felony crime to which you have plead guilty is at another level. For Scott, there was a very remote possibility of probation, but the reality was simply a question of how long he would be sentenced to prison.

1. Have you ever had a significant slice of your future life in someone else's hands?

    How do you handle uncertainty knowing it could be simply relief or it could be devastating and life altering?

    Read Matthew 6:25–34.
    What does it mean when Jesus said that if we seek Him, all the other things will work out?

    How would this bring comfort and courage?

    Read Philippians 4:6–7.
    Paul has been in prison several times when he wrote these words and was in jail at the time.

REFLECTION SECTION

How would God's promise of peace beyond understanding help you?

2. How do you handle knowing that one day all of us will have to stand before God?

   Read Hebrews 9:26–28.
   What alone can we cling to at that moment?

   How does the gravity of that moment put every other human judgment into perspective?

   Thought:
   The judge repeatedly exonerated Scott and commended him for his exemplary life. Though that did not completely change the outcome, it certainly gave Scott some affirmation that his attempts to live a Christ-honoring life were not in vain. He had done so many things right.

   How did that give Scott the strength to read his statement of confession?

3. Read again Scott's allocution, his statement of confession to the court (pp. 115–117).
   If you had to write one about your life to this point, what would you say?

Read Matthew 10:26.
Why is honesty so important?

Did reading Scott's statement give you higher regard for him or diminish him in your eyes?

What can you learn from that?

Read Luke 18:10–14.
Why was the tax collector justified before God?

Which is more significant—the number of our sins or the attitude of the sinner?

Close by reading 1 John 1:8–10, and thank Him for the gift of forgiveness.

REFLECTION SECTION

Section 5: Chapters 34–42
DESTINATION

1. How would you spend your time if you knew you were going to prison for four years in just two months?

Thought:
Scott took the time to be with his sons as much as possible, to go back to church even though not everyone there understood, and to craft a video that would lift up his story as a repentant sinner and be shown to the whole congregation.

Read again Scott's story as he told it on the video, summarizing his journey to that point (pp. 143–149).
Scott shares his struggle with two big issues—forgiveness and anger. Do these issues have a home in your life story?

Read Matthew 18:32–35.
Does Jesus's command to forgive make it any easier?

How have you struggled with forgiveness?

How does Jesus's prayer in Luke 23:34 set the bar for forgiveness?

Read Ephesians 4:26.
When we are angry with someone, how do we usually react?

What counsel does Paul give us here, and how could you live that out?

Thought:
God brought Tim, a fellow prisoner, into Scott's life for a very important reason—to settle the salvation issue once and for all. It seemed like everything Scott was experiencing—his correspondence Bible studies, the chapel services, and Tim's conversations—were all challenging him to lay everything down and ask Jesus to take complete control of his life. This was a monumental moment for Scott.

1 John 5:13 (NASB 1995) says, "These things I have written to you who believe in the name of the Son of God, so that you may know that you have eternal life."

Do you have this assurance?

What unfinished business do you need to deal with to bring you to this point?

Is there a "Tim" in your life who could help you?

Thought:
After Scott surrendered fully to Jesus, he began to study Scripture more and more, not out of duty but out of anticipation and joy. He looked forward to the time he could spend studying God's Word and began to grow as a Christian in many ways.

REFLECTION SECTION

Read John 8:47.
How important is God's Word in your life?

Are you growing in your hunger for the Word?

Read Psalm 119:9–16 (NASB 1995).
Look at the verbs concerning the Word. "Your word I have treasured in my heart." "I will meditate on your precepts." "I shall not forget Your word."

Are these characteristic of your attitude about studying God's Word?

If not, what could you do to change that?

End this session by reading Psalm 119:116 together aloud.

Section 6: Chapter 43
FORGIVENESS

Forgiveness is a two-way exchange. There is the forgiver, and there is the forgivee.

1. Have you been the forgivee? Have you hurt someone in the past and need to ask for their forgiveness?

    Read Romans 3:23.
    We have all sinned against God. Is it easier to ask God for forgiveness than other people?

    What is involved in asking other people for forgiveness?

2. Have you been the forgiver? Has someone hurt you, and you have held this hurt?

    Why is forgiving someone who hurt you so hard?

    Read: Matthew 6:14–15.
    What is this saying? How does it make you feel?

REFLECTION SECTION

Thought:

For most people, forgiving someone who has hurt them is a process. It is not like a light switch you can turn off. It is more like the dimmer switch that you slowly turn down over time. The first step in forgiving someone is the desire to forgive them because you need to forgive them—not just for them but for you.

Thought:

People try to forgive themselves. If you have done something and cannot forgive yourself, turn to God. Scripture does not encourage us to forgive ourselves but rather to put our faith and trust in the forgiveness of God for our sins.

www.ingramcontent.com/pod-product-compliance
Lightning Source LLC
Chambersburg PA
CBHW070532090426
42735CB00013B/2954